CURIOSITY
UNLEASHED

CURIOSITY UNLEASHED

Achieving Business Excellence by
Challenging the Status Quo

Dr. Diane Hamilton

Tampa, Florida

CURIOSITY UNLEASHED
Achieving Business Excellence by Challenging the Status Quo

Published by Gatekeeper Press
7853 Gunn Hwy., Suite 209
Tampa, FL 33626
www.GatekeeperPress.com

Library of Congress Control Number:

ISBN (hardcover): 9781662951602
ISBN (paperback): 9781662951619
eISBN: 9781662951626

For my current and future grandchildren.
My greatest hope is that you will remain curious.

FOREWORD

In a time marked by rapid technological innovation and intense global connectivity, the demands on businesses to continuously evolve and adapt have reached unprecedented levels. The digital age has not only accelerated change but also increased the complexity of the challenges we face. Throughout my career, from spearheading initiatives at Executive Networks to my early days shaping learning strategies, I have consistently observed that the foundation of enduring success in this dynamic environment is a steadfast commitment to fostering a culture of curiosity.

Curiosity Unleashed resonates with the very principles I have championed throughout my career. At Executive Networks, we have witnessed the power of curiosity in transforming not only business strategies but also in enriching leadership qualities. By encouraging leaders and employees alike to remain inquisitive about every facet of their environment, we cultivate a proactive rather than reactive approach to business challenges. *Curiosity Unleashed* provides a comprehensive exploration of this idea, backed by robust research and compelling case studies that illustrate the transformative power of curiosity in various organizational contexts.

Dr. Hamilton challenges the conventional wisdom that views curiosity merely as a whimsical trait, instead repositioning it as a strategic asset that drives innovation, enhances engagement, and ultimately, leads to profound organizational change.

As we navigate the complexities of the modern business world, the insights offered in *Curiosity Unleashed* are more pertinent than ever. It provides not only the inspiration but also the practical guidance necessary for embedding curiosity into the DNA of corporate culture. Dr. Hamilton's stories connect deeply with my experiences and observations, highlighting curiosity's role in unlocking creativity, encouraging risk-taking, and fostering an environment where learning and growth are at the forefront.

I wholeheartedly recommend *Curiosity Unleashed* to leaders, change-makers, and professionals across all industries who are eager to lead their organizations into new frontiers of success. This book will equip you with the knowledge and tools to harness the boundless potential of curiosity, turning everyday challenges into opportunities for innovation. Let it inspire you to challenge conventional boundaries and lead with curiosity, transforming your professional environment and achieving enduring success in our rapidly changing world.

Mike Dulworth
Founder and CEO
Executive Networks, Inc.

TABLE OF CONTENTS

PART I

WHAT WE KNOW

PROLOGUE

Curiosity books are much like emotional intelligence books: those who need them likely won't read them. So let me commend you for being curious enough to read this one!

This book takes up where my previous book, *Cracking the Curiosity Code* (2019), left off; it dives deeper into the value of curiosity and includes examples of individuals and organizations who have benefitted financially from developing curiosity as well as examples of those who have failed by not doing so. Most importantly, it explains how to overcome the barriers that inhibit curiosity.

Additionally, this book shares with you what I have taught to the thousands who have taken my training courses and attended my presentations. I hope that as you read *Curiosity Unleashed*, you too will realize the value of curiosity and how its definition can vary, and also come to appreciate its key role in both organizational and individual development.

I have divided this book into multiple sections so that readers can easily access whatever topic interests them most. Section one opens the book with insights into curiosity gleaned from some of the incredible guests I have interviewed on my long-running radio program, *Take the Lead*.

The second section addresses the financial benefits that come from fostering curiosity. Leaders might find this the most critical section to read because it explores how low curiosity often correlates with various challenges that organizations face. Curiosity is the driving force behind innovation, engagement, communication, motivation, and overall productivity.

The third section presents examples of successful organizations that embraced curiosity and embedded it in their core cultural values. It also highlights the financial rewards these organizations have reaped.

The fourth section delves into intriguing products and instances that have sparked curiosity in the natural world or within organizations. It features stories of notable companies that have embraced curiosity and created world-class products as a result.

The fifth section explores the impact of artificial intelligence (AI) on the future of curiosity and addresses AI's potential benefits and risks. This section also discusses issues related to job security and artificial curiosity and their implications.

Although this book primarily focuses on developing curiosity at work, section six delves into how curiosity can affect personal considerations such as passion, life alignment, experiential balance, and individual growth.

Section seven showcases the stories of well-known individuals globally recognized for their inquisitive nature and discusses how they leveraged curiosity to succeed.

Section eight shares examples of organizations that clung to the status quo—much to their detriment.

Section nine provides key insights for those seeking to enhance curiosity within themselves or their organization. It shares findings on inhibiting factors and introduces the Curiosity Code Index (CCI), the first assessment to identify four factors that can impede curiosity: fear, assumptions, technology, and environment (FATE).

The final section empowers readers to take actionable steps and offers concrete suggestions on how to use curiosity to unlock both personal and organizational success.

Let the exploration begin!

Diane

INTRODUCTION

When it comes to curiosity, the foreword to *Cracking the Curiosity Code* holds a special place for me, having been written by my friend Keith Krach, the former Chairman and CEO of DocuSign and former Under Secretary of State for Economic Growth, Energy, and the Environment. Krach, the embodiment of curiosity in action, set the tone for that book.

When I interviewed Keith and thousands of other notable leaders for my nationally-syndicated radio show and podcast, I found curiosity to be a recurring theme—even though I hadn't intended to make it the central topic of the show. As these guests have provided me with some of my most insightful lessons on curiosity, I transcribed those interviews, preserving their conversational flow, and have placed the resulting nuggets at the beginning of this book. I hope they pique your interest in curiosity and entice you to read the rest of the book. Most of all, I hope that you find their insights as inspiring as I have!

*　*　*

DANIEL GOLEMAN,
psychologist and author of *Emotional Intelligence*

I asked Daniel: So, have you always been a curious person?

Daniel's Response: Curiosity is one reason I left psychology and went into journalism. I was at the *Times* for twelve years, some of it spent in the science department. In journalism, whatever catches your fancy and might be of interest to other people, you can pursue. I found psychology departments weren't that open, frankly. There are two strategies that companies and people generally use in life. One is exploit and the other is explore. Psychology departments, at least in my experience, wanted me to exploit. They wanted me to refine a topic that I could spin around and add something to. It's a bit like a company that has a product that makes money that they tweak every year so that it keeps bringing in the cash. To explore, on the other hand, means to be curious, to look around, and to find something new. Schopenhauer said, "Genius is hitting the target others do not see." Steve Jobs was fantastic at that. He may not have been so great in other ways, but that was one strength that he had. And it showed in Apple. I found in journalism that you could explore widely. I never thought about that before, but now that you pointed it out, I can see that I was curious.

I can see why you've developed a measure of curiosity. You're very curious. I remember an article in the *Harvard Business Review* by Claudio Fernández-Aráoz saying that curiosity is one of the key competencies in the future. You're ahead of the game.

* * *

TOM PETERS,
author of *In Search of Excellence*

I asked Tom: Where does curiosity fall on your list of important traits?

Tom's Response: Curiosity to me is about people who are interested in everything. Because to me, curiosity is horizontal, not vertical. Horizontal—and I was tweeting about this—is one of the reasons I have been in a tech firm and have 23 code writers working for me. I want one theater major, I want one music major, I want one philosophy major, and I want somebody who is as bright as the dickens but for family reasons never did make it through formal schooling.

I read an exchange on Twitter where somebody related how they knew a guy who had worked for the CIA as part of a sophisticated operation. The guy who had worked for the CIA said that when he put teams together, he always looked for somebody who had a musical background because she or he would come at the problem differently. That to me is the essence of curiosity; somebody who is thinking about Bach while you're thinking about third derivative calculus equations.

I said another thing that relates to all of this, and it also has to do with what curiosity is (and this may change in a few years), and it is that there are no experts. You have to experiment. You have to figure it out for yourself. As with any new product, you're going to make 173 mistakes before you get a ritual that works. I know there will be 257.6 books about how to work from home within a few years, but now there aren't, and we need to play with it. Acknowledge to your teammates that you're playing with it. Say to them, "This Zoom thing is new to me. I have no idea in the world what we're doing. I have no other idea whether this is going to be a bust or genius, but we'll all try."

I have to tell you another tiny story that I read on Twitter, which is relevant to our conversation. When I read it, I almost got ill because I laughed so hard. Let's say that I'm a salesperson, male, you are a customer, female. I want to learn more about your needs, so I ask you questions. I ask you four questions, and you reply each time, but in the middle of your reply I always interrupt you. I ask a fifth question, but you just sit there and don't say anything. Finally, I say, "Aren't you going to answer?" and you say, "You always answer your own questions anyway, so I thought I'd wait."

* * *

DOUG CONANT,
former President and CEO of the Campbell Soup Company

I asked Doug: How much do you think curiosity ties into improving engagement?

Doug's Response: It's huge. I'm going to bridge over into some of Jim Collins's work with his Level 5 Leadership model. He talked about what to differentiate. He was surprised at some of the lessons he learned when he wrote *Good to Great: Why Some Companies Make the Leap and Others Don't*. When he was writing his book, he expected that many of the leaders would be hard-charging, Jack Welch [the former CEO of GE] types. But the ones he met he had never heard of. He said, "What's going on here?" As he did the work and he did his Level 5 Leadership model, he said, "There are two distinguishing characteristics here. One is they have a fierce desire to advance the enterprise. It's not about themselves; it's about advancing the enterprise."

The second thing he said is that they have great humility. They're always curious. They're always asking questions. They don't have all the answers, and they know it. They share that with everybody, saying, "What do you think? How could we do this better?" This goes back to 2000. When I heard Jim talking about it, I was thinking that that makes so much sense to me because in my heart of hearts I had all the answers, but in my heart of hearts, I was a new CEO, and I didn't have all the answers. I found there was much more power in bringing more humility to the conversation and asking more questions. We placed a premium on curiosity and how we can do things better.

A thousand years ago, when I was at Kraft, I had a boss who had this line. I didn't understand it at the time, but I do now—I'm a little slow. He would say, "Doug, better is always best." His point was to focus on continuous improvement and constantly try to do better. We could become paralyzed while pursuing being the best. Let's do a little better now than we did before. Continuous improvement is the way of the world because large organizations can't make giant changes on a dime. It's all a continuous improvement process. The only way continuous improvement works is if there is unlimited curiosity in the environment.

I asked Doug: Even if you're a curious person as a leader, how do you get your employees to be more curious?

Doug's Response: This is my personal philosophy. I talk about my leadership model, the heart of which is honor people and inspire trust. I find that high-trust cultures create high-curiosity cultures. I've read all the books on fear, including *Only the Paranoid Survive: How to Exploit the Crisis Points That Challenge Every Company.* I've been in a lot of fear-based cultures and paranoid cultures, and I don't find them to have an endless supply of curiosity. Fear and intimidation is a slippery slope. You may create a breakthrough every once in a while because people are so paranoid that they come up with a breakthrough idea. But in the fullness of time, the way you create a curious culture is to create a high-trust culture where people can feel safe even when they are vulnerable. Because if you feel vulnerable, you can't create a high-curiosity culture.

I go back to the notion that all roads lead to trust. Stephen M.R. Covey wrote a book, *The Speed of Trust*, and he gave it the best subtitle of all time. He said, "It's the one thing that changes everything." If I'm on a high-trust team, I don't care how dire the situation is. I know that we're going to find a way to get through it. If I'm on a low-trust team, I know we're not going anywhere. I buy the notion that when you create a high-trust culture your odds of having a more innovative and more curious culture go up exponentially. That's the path I traveled to get to curiosity.

* * *

AMY EDMONDSON,
Professor of Leadership at Harvard Business School

I asked Amy: If leaders don't recognize that they're not going to be innovative unless they let people ask questions and provide content, what is the best way to get leaders to help others to speak their minds?

Amy's Response: It starts with helping leaders to recognize to be mindful of what we're up against. Many managers have a taken-for-granted mental model. I don't think very much about it. It's just my mental model, but there's work to be done, and people won't do it unless they're motivated to do it. They should be a little bit afraid of what will happen if they don't do it. It's like, "What do I need to do to get people to work hard?" is the question they're asking, rather than "What do I need to do to get people to work smart and thoughtfully? How do I help people bring their great ideas and their full selves to work? How do I foster ingenuity, creativity, learning, innovation?" Those things do not happen in a fear-based culture. They simply don't. Neuroscience research has shown us that when people are afraid, they have fewer cognitive resources available for such things as short-term memory and creativity.

We know that fear doesn't help us do what we have to do, but we forget this. Managers forget to take that seriously and think, "What's the nature of the work we're going to do? How do I have to show up to help people do that well?" It starts with reminding themselves of the VUCA [volatility, uncertainty, complexity, and ambiguity] world that we live in. We need people asking questions and offering ideas and acknowledging failures rather than just buckling down and working hard because that won't get you anywhere. It starts with them recognizing the nature of the work and then being willing to remind other people of the nature of the work. They must make the logical case for the voice for why their input is both needed and expected.

Silence doesn't announce itself. You don't know when people are holding back because there's no thought bubble above their head that you can see. What does that mean? What are the implications of that? To learn what people hold back, we must ask questions. There is power in good questions. You're constantly reminding yourself that your job is to be curious, and if your job is to be curious, then you had better ask questions. You better ask good questions, meaning the kind of questions that you genuinely know you don't have answers for. The kind of questions that help people focus thoughtfully on a particular situation or issue. They're not questions like, "What's on your mind?" They're questions like, "What do you think about this project?" "What are the risks here with this topic?" "Are they focusing on us enough?" They're not yes or no questions. They're not overly narrow. They don't give us a multiple-choice response. A good question helps us focus and gives us room to respond. A good question expresses curiosity, and it also engenders curiosity in others.

*   *   *

ALBERT BANDURA,
one of the world's most influential social psychologists.

I asked Albert: Do you think curiosity comes before or after motivation?

Albert Response: Curiosity would be a source of motivation. To get curious, you better start examining a lot of things.

I asked Albert: It sounds like your mother had a big impact on your curiosity and your sense of needing to have an education; would you agree?

Albert's Response: That was interesting because in this small town, about 90% of the male youngsters became farmers. The principal of the school called my parents in, and she said, "I gave your son this test called the IQ test. I don't think Albert should be a farmer. I think he should go to college." My parents said, "We don't have any money." She said, "You will find the money, but you have to make the decision that he isn't going to be a farmer and that he should go to college." That was another impetus. My parents didn't have any education, but they've put a tremendous emphasis on self-development through education. I also acknowledge the value of curiosity because it is what led me to do my research at Stanford.

*   *   *

ROBERT CIALDINI, professor
and author of *Influence: The Psychology of Persuasion*

I asked Robert: In my research, I found that environment has a big influence on your curiosity; would you agree?

Robert's Response: That's a great insight. My clients will sometimes ask, "What should I be looking for? What's the one trait I should be looking for in a salesperson?" My answer is empathy, somebody who doesn't judge what is the most appropriate or likely effective approach in this situation by self-reflection or looking inside themselves but by empathizing with the market. Who are the people that you're speaking to? What are they likely to resonate with? What are they most likely to find congruent with the way they like to make their choices? Empathy is that ability to get out of yourself, put yourself into their shoes, into the head of the people that you're trying to influence that makes you the superior persuasive communicator.

I asked Robert: Do you need curiosity to build empathy so that you know which questions to ask to get there?

Robert's Response: It's curiosity seasoned with self-interest. If you know the right questions to ask, you're going to be more successful in that process.

I asked Robert: How do you know the right questions to ask?

Robert's Response: You know the right questions to ask by looking into the situation and seeing what's available for you in that situation. I claim that there are seven universal principles of influence. One of them is authority. Another is social proof.

Another is scarcity. When you investigate the situation, are there true authorities whose opinion you can point to that support your position? Use that and bring that to prominence.

Is there true consensus or popularity associated with what you are offering that's essentially social proof? Bring that to the surface. Is there a genuine dwindling opportunity or uniqueness about that scarcity? Bring that to the surface. You never treat these people unethically. You are simply pointing to something in the situation that already exists.

You're not counterfeiting it or manufacturing it in any way that is dishonest. Both sides benefit from knowing about true authority, knowing true popularity, seizing genuine, scarce opportunities, and so on. Who loses under those circumstances? I don't think anybody loses. As a result, you have a long-term partner. Somebody who is likely to want to come back to you the next time they're interested in a commercial exchange.

* * *

JIM MCKELVEY,
co-founder of Block and Square

I asked Jim: As we discuss curiosity, is there any other quality or difference between being a regular businessperson or entrepreneur that you want to focus on?

Jim's Response: If we're going to use a historic definition of an entrepreneur, which is somebody who's doing something totally new, then there are certain traits that help you. Curiosity is absolutely key. I would say that humility, which is a cousin of curiosity, is also key. You can't be curious if you think you already know. Arrogance kills curiosity quicker than anything else. As soon as humans are certain what the answer is, they turn off. It was amazing to me because we're told that entrepreneurs are somehow bold, adventurous, devil-may-care people. A lot of them are very humble, curious, and scared. This is another interesting thing. Most of them didn't want to be entrepreneurs. Most of them got unlucky and found themselves in a terrible situation where the normal stuff that used to work no longer worked. They were in this horrible situation, and they adapted it by building an innovation stack and they ended up becoming titans of industry.

* * *

ROGER MARTIN,
former Dean at the Rotman School of Management, named the World's #1 Management Thinker by Thinkers50

I asked Roger: Do you have any examples of companies that have utilized curiosity to overcome status quo thinking?

Roger's Response: Before diving into examples, I can also say that the techniques that I use to stop people from getting negative quickly on an idea is my favorite question, which you may have read it, which is "What would have to be true?" If you were to say to me, "Roger, this would be a great idea," rather than say, "What's your data to support it? Can you prove that to me?" I say, "Let's do a little exercise. Let's figure out what would have to be true for that to be the awesome idea you think it is. What would have to be true about customers? What would have to be true about the distribution channels? What would have to be true about potential competitors? What would have to be true about our capabilities? What would have to be true about the cost structure?" You build a picture of the things that would have to be true for that to be a good idea.

If you ask, "Are those things true?" and the answer is mainly "No," you can say, "What would we have to do to make each of those things true?" Customers have never heard of this. What would we have to do? We'd have to create some programs that enable people who would be consumers out there to experience it. We have to sample it or do this or that or whatever. What I try to do is make it into a creative exercise by asking the question, "Can we make enough things true to say this is a good idea? Can we imagine a plan to make enough things true?" That keeps it in the positive domain rather than evaluation by way of essential critique and looking at the shortfalls. It's an evaluation by looking at what I call the happy story.

Tell me a happy story of what this would look like, and then let's work backward from the happy story to say what stuff we would have to do to make that happy story come true. For example, I had the great privilege of working with one of the smartest women I've ever met, Tina Brown, on the turnaround of *The New Yorker* magazine. She famously turned around *Vanity Fair* and then was given the tough job of saving *The New Yorker*, which was losing money and sliding dramatically.

One of the challenges of *The New Yorker* was what it had been. At one time, it was absolutely the dominant magazine. In terms of selling ads, it had all the highest dollars per page in all metrics, but it no longer had those advantages and was struggling. If the Condé Nast folks hadn't bought it, it probably would long since have succumbed. We had to think about how you could get people to pay high rates for ad pages, because when you looked at the demographics of *The New Yorker* reader, they weren't as rich as people think they were. They weren't as urban as people think, either. They're a mix of men and women, about 50/50, which is the worst mix you want for magazines because advertisers would much rather have either a woman's magazine or a man's magazine. It's not that one gender is better than the other, but a 50/50 mix is the worst.

We had to come up with what is it about *The New Yorker* readers that would cause you to want to pay a higher premium, higher CPMs per viewer than you would for a competitor's. It occurred to me that there *is* something different about *New Yorker* readers than the reader of an average magazine, which is that the *New Yorker* reader is a curious person who's interested in the latest thinking across a whole bunch of domains. If you read *The New Yorker*, you will see articles about politics, science, sports, all kinds of books, everything under the sun.

That's also bad for advertisers too because they'd rather have a magazine's audience and content be targeted. At a cocktail party or a dinner, who is everybody going to be listening to? It's going to be *The New Yorker* reader who is currently looking for the most interesting subjects of the day, regardless of the topic. What is *The New Yorker*? *The New Yorker* is the perfect launch vehicle. If you're advertising the next *upgrade* of this car or that car, then no, but if you're launching a brand-new SUV, a brand-new drug, a brand-new movie, a brand-new whatever, then you need *The New Yorker*. This is not hype. This is absolutely true. Part of the turnover of *The New Yorker* was selling it as the launch vehicle and selling to advertisers who are launching something new and distinct and who needed to generate buzz. The way to generate buzz about something was to have *The New Yorker* readers know about it, think about it.

* * *

ZANDER LURIE,
CEO of SurveyMonkey

I asked Zander: How did you get to this level of appreciating curiosity?

Zander's Response: I am psyched to talk to you partly because you are a curious person. That is the mission of the company: to power the curious. Our products and software help individuals and organizations. It's for curious people who want to serve their customers, their employees, and the new markets they're going after better. The best thing you can do is ask other human beings for their opinions. For people who want to take that rich sentiment data, opinion data, and marry it to the other data they have, we believe those are the people that launched the best products, marketing campaigns, packaging, pricing, student benefits, and health care. Curiosity is at the root of all human beings. All parents know that children are inherently curious and happy. Then that curiosity gets rooted out of you when you're told what to do, what's right, and what constitutes smart.

Our products are about infusing curiosity into the workflows in your companies, institutions, and nonprofit. That's the brand we get psyched to serve seventeen million active users every day and over 650,000 paid customers. #PowerTheCurious is what SurveyMonkey does. We created the category seventeen years ago and the company is thriving now.

There are certain things that you need to focus on to make a curious workplace.

I asked Zander: So, how do you go about making a curious workplace at SurveyMonkey?

Zander's Response: Curiosity is at the heart of innovation. We embrace curiosity through asking questions and being disruptive to be better. We like to think we are in the relentless self-improvement business. How can we help make our products more productive for our customers? How can we make an environment here at SurveyMonkey so that people can do the best work of their lives? We've had to be very prescriptive in terms of how we run the business. For starters, we don't embrace individuals who interrupt and feel like they have this inherent right to demand their opinion be accepted, just because they're more senior to other people. We're trying to embrace a collaborative culture where we have direct conversations. We give honest feedback. We celebrate asking people for feedback, asking people for growth opportunities, development opportunities, and celebrating good questions that challenge the status quo.

We've implemented mentorship programs. I do a lot of skip-level meetings with folks who report to my directs to understand what's working on their team. If you look at SurveyMonkey, we're not the place where you get your annual review, and once a year you find out how you're doing. This is a place where there is constant feedback. We're constantly using our product to assess how we can be better. I like to use one example just because we've put some press around it. We think it's important. We do an annual check in on our benefits, where we can allocate money to be more productive with our employee base. When we surveyed our 800-plus employees months ago, some of the unstructured feedback came back asking how we are treating our contractors—the janitors to clean our bathrooms, the chefs who work in our kitchen. There are dozens of people here who are primarily immigrants who are not in the highest paying jobs asking about their parental leave policies, their vacation days, and bereavement leave.

We found out that we were not paying these people the same high-quality benefits that we're offering our designers, engineers, and sales folks. We implemented the same benefits package for our contractors as we do for our full-time employees. We asked the vendors who employ those contractors to kick in, and if they didn't kick in, we were not going to keep working with them. Those kinds of benefits did not come from my creativity or good ideas. It was born out of a survey of our employees. It goes to show you that soliciting input from a diverse group of people who work around you can bring the best ideas to the floor. We implemented those. Our employee base celebrated those. We put some PR around it, and we see other companies following suit, which we are super proud of.

*   *   *

While many captivating guests have shared how they infused curiosity into their workplace, I had room to select only a handful for this introduction; their wisdom alone could fill an entire book. If you have a curious mind and wish to explore further insights, you can find transcripts of these conversations at https:/drdianehamilton.com/blog.

CHAPTER 1

Shedding Status-Quo Thinking

There is some comfort in the thought that we will never know everything. It would be a very dull universe for any intelligent being were everything of importance to be known.

—Carl Sagan

The amount of attention given to the value of curiosity has changed since I wrote *Cracking the Curiosity Code*. Through years of giving the Curiosity Code Index (CCI) assessment, I have watched the lightbulbs go off over people's heads as they recognized what has held them back from their natural passion for exploring and asking questions.

This led to my desire to write *Curiosity Unleashed*. In this book I wanted to share what I learned from the people who went through my training programs and attended events where I spoke. I received many terrific questions from people who wanted to build their curiosity but weren't sure how.

Whether they wanted to know how to question their boss without coming across as confrontational, how to incorporate a curiosity-based culture, or how to answer a wealth of other questions and concerns, I recognized that I needed to write a book specifically on how to develop curiosity in the modern workplace as well as how to develop it personally.

I consider *Cracking the Curiosity Code* essential reading because it discusses the history and importance of curiosity. It also discusses how curiosity peaks when we are children and falls off dramatically as we age.

Curiosity is not unique to humans. The Max Planck Institute coined the term "curiosity gene" based on its work researching a songbird. Consider the bird who does not embrace curiosity. If it flies around a bush looking for berries but does not explore any other bushes, the bird will die once the berries run out.

There are endless examples of work-related reasons to improve curiosity. On a personal level, rewarding curiosity triggers dopamine, which makes us feel good.

What drove my research was my frustration that very little had been written about curiosity, which is so valuable and critical to the success, both financial and otherwise, of individuals and organizations, and about the connection between developing curiosity and the financial benefits that development can yield. I was also frustrated that very little had been written about the factors that inhibit curiosity. This frustrated me because leaders often like to see quantifiable data to make changes. At the same time, I didn't want to present reams of dry, numerical data and research, which are often uninteresting to many people. Therefore, I strived to share these connections through success stories and examples.

In this book, I have continued to highlight highly successful business leaders, innovative entrepreneurs, and, most importantly, share the intricate findings of the scientific community regarding curiosity.

Since I published my last book, artificial intelligence (AI) has taken off dramatically. Will this technology help or hinder curiosity? Could it provide all the answers? The Internet can only tell us what we already know, so we will need curious individuals to provide the content needed to fuel AI.

But what precisely was holding back the organizations that clung to unsuccessful ways? Why were they hesitant to embrace curiosity? Some factors included risk aversion, too much focus on immediate results, fear of losing control, traditional hierarchical structures, unfamiliarity with curiosity's impact and value, the belief that curiosity is a distraction, and clinging to short-term goals rather than looking at opportunity costs.

Some of the most successful individuals have recognized that embracing curiosity is critical for breaking free from the chains of that negative dialogue.

*   *   *

Even though many consider Elon Musk a polarizing figure, I've included him in this book. *Fortune Magazine* noted that ambiguity when it published an article titled "Why Critics Love to Hate Elon Musk—and Why His Fans Adore Him."

On my long drives I often listen to audiobooks to learn about leaders who embrace or fail to embrace curiosity. On a recent drive, I listened to Walter Isaacson's book, *Elon Musk*. Although he shared endless examples of Musk's curiosity, one particular story interested me.

While developing SpaceX, Musk focused on keeping costs down by always questioning whether it was better to create the company's own supplies or purchase from manufacturers. He learned that many rocket components were expensive because they required hundreds of specifications dictated by the military and NASA. He and his team questioned each specification, keeping only those he deemed "decreed by the laws of physics."

He further questioned the status quo when he bought GoPro cameras off the shelf to use for the cameras mounted on the rockets—they were much cheaper than the custom-designed cameras typically used in aerospace. In another instance, he found it cheaper to design and build his own flight computers, which cost him around $10,000 but would have cost around $100,000 had he sourced them from traditional aerospace man-ufacturers. Musk is famous for saying that the best part was no part, meaning that he and his team strove constantly to simplify designs to keep costs down. Additionally, he moved away from the wasteful cost-plus contracts that he thought stifled innovation. Musk did what many leaders should have done when he questioned the status quo. While he may be more fearless than most, others can do as he did to help their company survive and succeed.

Why do some individuals, like Elon Musk, thrive on curiosity, while others shy away from it? That is what intrigued me. To find out, I interviewed thousands of successful entrepreneurs and leaders and spoke with presidential hopefuls as well as founders of unicorn organizations, asking each one how and why they embraced curiosity. Their curiosity led them down different paths—some successful, some not. Even if they regretted their past failures, they all shared that those failures eventually made them successful. They learned to fail forward.

Even Musk has faced setbacks on his path to wealth, making his ride less than smooth. For instance, he was replaced as CEO while at PayPal, and he had multiple rockets blow up before having one launch successfully at SpaceX. He has also admitted that Tesla was about a month away from bankruptcy during the launch of his Model 3, which he called a "production and logistics hell."

Ultimately, however, his passion for curiosity has helped make him the wealthiest man in the world.

* * *

To improve our curiosity, we need mentorship. You might not be able to have Elon Musk as your mentor, but you can learn from his experiences. When choosing mentors with whom we can interact, finding those who have done what we have yet to do is critical. Too often I see people surround themselves with people who are just like them, and when they do this, they miss the opportunity to learn from those who are different from them.

My experience as an advisor at the Global Mentor Network (part of the Krach Institute for Tech Diplomacy at Purdue) was invaluable. GMN is the brainchild of Keith Krach, former Under Secretary of State, CEO, and Chairman of DocuSign, and Thuy Vu, former reporter and seven-time Emmy Award winner. The goal of GMN is to create mentorship at scale. As part of their podcast, I had the pleasure of interviewing some of the top chief human resource officers (CHROs) in the world. These leaders determined their organizations' culture and training. Whether they worked at Encore Capital, Juniper, The Real Real, Comerica, Cardinal Health, DocuSign, or some other successful organization, these leaders embraced curiosity and sought ways to replace status-quo thinking.

Most leaders I interviewed had had a valuable mentor in their life. Even famous successful people I didn't interview have had mentors. Musk was mentored by Larry Page, the co-founder of Google. Steve Jobs was inspired by Robert Noyce, the co-founder of Intel, and Mark Zuckerberg was inspired by Steve Jobs.

Not all mentors must be CEOs of Fortune 500 organizations. Oprah Winfrey often credits Maya Angelou as her mentor, and Sheryl Sandberg received insights from former Treasury Secretary and Harvard president Larry Summers.

While mentors and role models can foster curiosity in those they mentor, so too can our curiosity be fostered by many factors. These can include education and books, literature, music and the arts, experiences of all kinds, personal connections, and collaborations. Other factors that foster curiosity might be failure and adversity, exposure to new ideas, self-reflection, exposure to other cultures and lifestyles, and access to technology. In this book, we will consider many paths to improving curiosity. However, to walk down those paths, we must first examine what keeps us from taking that first step.

When you look back at the goals you've accomplished (and those you haven't), consider what has held you back. If you lacked curiosity but didn't know how to harness it, this book will help guide you.

According to Steward Friedman, Emeritus Professor of Management Practice at the Wharton School of Business, curiosity and the ability to question the status quo are essential leadership skills that can be learned.

When I began writing *Cracking the Curiosity Code*, I had no idea that journey would take me down a rabbit hole of exploration that would lead to the creation of something so much more significant. I was always intrigued—and sometimes frustrated—by people who did not seem interested in exploring ideas, getting to the bottom of things, and finding out why and how things worked. I learned from having taught thousands of business classes that many of my students wanted me to hand them a fish rather than teach them to fish. I believed that writing a book about curiosity could help them. I didn't think I'd need to do more than write a book. However, I also wanted to fix the problem of what inhibited curiosity. How can you overcome issues if you do not know what inhibits you?

Because I had written my doctoral dissertation on the impact of emotional intelligence on performance, I was familiar with assessments. However, when I searched far and wide for an assessment to determine what kept people from being curious, I found none. Some assessments, like Todd Kashdan's, determine levels of curiosity and measure whether you are highly curious or not, but they don't determine what might be keeping you from being curious. So, even if those assessments can uncover if the training and development you use are helping foster curiosity, they provide no insight into what inhibits people from being curious, or how to improve curiosity. That is why I created the Curiosity Code Index (CCI), the first-ever assessment that gauges the factors that hamper curiosity. That decision changed not only my life but potentially millions of lives.

Improving curiosity is the most important thing we can do to create a more engaged, innovative, and productive workplace. Just as Daniel Goleman popularized the value of emotional intelligence, I believed that someone needed to do the same for curiosity. When Goleman was on my radio show, he stated that he believed curiosity was *the* critical competency of the future. I could not agree more.

However, curiosity is a broad term and can be hard to define because it means many things to different people. And since I talk a lot about curiosity, I am often asked to define it. Is it about asking questions? Is it about exploring the unexplored? Is it about wanting to learn new things? My answer: Yes, yes, and yes! But again, it is far more than that.

My definition kept changing until I uncovered what I was really helping people do: escape status-quo thinking. To me, curiosity is about not doing the same thing over and over without questioning why or exploring other alternatives.

My efforts focus primarily on the workplace (though I also cover the personal realm). And as I researched curiosity within organizations, I kept running into organizations that unknowingly embraced status-quo behaviors. Consider Xerox, for example. When I was a secretary in the 1980s, Xerox ruled the photocopying world. Their position was so dominant, in fact, that their very name became synonymous with the act of photocopying; the word Xerox (like Google) became a verb.

After pioneering the photocopying industry, however, Xerox began to fear that a paperless office would someday put them out of business. In response, they founded the Xerox Palo Alto Research Center (aka Xerox PARC) where, by the late 1970s, they had developed ground-breaking technologies that included the graphical user interface (GUI) and the computer mouse. With its focus still on copying, Xerox failed to commercialize these innovations and continued to invest heavily in the photocopier business. Fatefully, a young man toured Xerox PARC during this time and was enthralled with their developments, especially the GUI. You may know his name: Steve Jobs, the founder of Apple. In short order, Apple, and later Microsoft, used Xerox's innovations to create the personal computer, all while Xerox continued to lose its market position in photocopying. Had Xerox embraced a culture of curiosity, it could have seen the opportunity sitting right in front of them and recognized an emerging market. Instead, Xerox continued to struggle with status-quo thinking and was eventually acquired by Fujifilm for $6 billion in 2018. (In contrast, Apple's market capitalization as of this writing is approaching $3 trillion.)

Another industry that suffered from relying on status-quo ways is bookstores, one of the most successful of which was Borders Books. Founded in 1971, by the mid-1970s Borders had become a significant player in the retail book business. By the 2000s, however, the publishing industry had begun to change as more and more customers bought books online at Amazon, which itself had become a powerhouse. Borders and other brick-and-mortar bookstores failed to transition quickly to offering online retailing. Upset at having to do their job without the aid of available technology, Borders' employees complained about their work/life balance because Borders had failed to make their employees' jobs less difficult. This, combined with poor communication from leadership, caused employee engagement to reach an all-time low. Borders' poor vision also led them to contract their e-commerce business out to Amazon, their biggest competitor. Even that poor response was too little too late, and in 2011, sixteen years after becoming a public company, Borders filed for bankruptcy and closed all their stores. In the end, Borders had wrongly believed that their customers no longer loved books when in reality their customers simply preferred having more than one way to buy them. As the world around Borders changed, they failed to respond. One has to wonder what Borders would look like today had they asked questions and been more curious.

Technology grows and changes quickly, and the organizations that embrace those changes can thrive. Remember the first PalmPilots? Can you remember the last time you even saw one? Palm Inc., the company that produced them, experienced success with their PalmPilot in the 1990s. However, when the mobile industry evolved, Palm Inc. failed to transition their product to compete with what smartphones were offering. Their PDAs lacked the smartphone's new and innovative features and their design was much less sleek than their competitors'. Palm Inc. tried to respond but struggled with delays in product releases. That, combined with their limited apps, marketing challenges, stiff competition from Apple and Google, and a lack of adaptability, resulted in their demise; in 2010 they were acquired by Hewlett-Packard for $1.2 billion. As much as early adopters enjoyed exploring those first PalmPilots, those same early adopters abandoned them when competitors produced designs that worked better and held more promise. Lacking a culture of curiosity, a once-innovative organization turned into one that lacked relevance.

Palm Inc. was not the only organization that clung to status-quo ways. In the 70s and 80s, Radio Shack had a store in just about every mall and in every city. While their products weren't high end, they did a steady business catering to hobbyists and audiophiles on a budget. Founded in 1921 and later acquired by Tandy Corporation, Radio Shack grew over time to become *the* dominant electronics retailer. And then something happened.

Larger, big box retailers like Circuit City and Best Buy, as well as other regional offerings, sprung up and started to encroach on Radio Shack's market. Online retail soon followed, further decreasing Radio Shack's market share. Faced with these challenges, Radio Shack failed to materially respond, mustering only a few weak and inconsistent efforts at rebranding that only further confused their target customers. As a result, their customer base further declined. In short, a curious population lost interest due to a company's dated approach. The end finally came in a 2015 bankruptcy; Radio Shack never fully recovered. When customers don't understand what a company offers, they go elsewhere. Curiosity is critical to help determine how best to reach and continue to engage with your customers. And so to keep your customers coming to you for their needs, you must change, innovate, and communicate clearly—all of which happens with curiosity.

Sometimes an organization communicates clearly, but their product becomes obsolete. When I was younger, Tower Records was *the* destination for music enthusiasts and was considered the cool place to get your music. Founded in 1960, it quickly became the dominant record retailer. By the early 2000s, however, the digital revolution changed the industry dramatically, and physical formats declined in popularity. The shift also caused morale and motivational issues for Tower Records' employees as they resisted adapting to a new business model in order to remain competitive. Tower's leadership should have involved employees in proactively responding to the revolution. Had they fostered an organization of change and helped employees find their own way to embrace digital formats, things might have gone better for the giant. Instead, Tower filed for bankruptcy in 2006. These examples shed light on what often happens when organizations fail to embrace a culture of curiosity. Escaping the status quo is not always easy, but it can generate fresh perspectives, creative thinking, adaptability, problem-solving, and continuous improvement—all of which can lead to motivation, engagement, innovation, and a competitive advantage. Developing curiosity is more than just learning and development. It means shedding status-quo behaviors so we can alter our perspective, become more empathetic, and better align with new opportunities as we create a life of unlimited potential.

To break free of status-quo thinking, individuals and organizations must recognize that curiosity is the spark that will ignite all they hope to achieve.

CHAPTER 2

The Spark that Ignites Most Organizational Issues

It's through curiosity and looking at opportunities in new ways that we've always mapped our path at Dell. There's always an opportunity to make a difference.

—Michael Dell

Why is developing curiosity so important? Because it ties into everything we hope to fix in our professional and our personal lives. It might help to think of curiosity as the spark that ignites the process: like the first scene of any *Mission Impossible* movie, that fuse leads to an explosion—in this case a positive one. Fail to light the match, however, and we just have a fuse, which would be quite a dull opening for the movie! In the same way, failing to light the spark of curiosity can lead to a dull and unproductive life.

So, what can the match of curiosity ignite? Nearly everything! I like to compare the process to baking a cake. For instance, if you mix eggs, milk, flour, and other ingredients and pour them into a pan and place it into the oven, not much will happen until you turned on the oven. To be innovative and productive in the workplace, we must consider the spark. Because when we ignite the spark of curiosity, we ignite motivation, drive, engagement, creativity, communication, and all of the other soft skills that we hope to improve. The problem comes when companies merely mix the ingredients without first turning on the oven. When we start in the middle of the process, no one gets cake.

In *Cracking the Curiosity Code*, I wrote about what happens to our natural curiosity levels as we age. For this book, suffice it to say that we are born with high levels of curiosity that peak around the age of five and then diminish dramatically as we grow older.

That same peak and drop happens to creativity as well. In his incredible TED talk about whether schools kill creativity, Sir Ken Robinson acknowledged that we have created an educational system that educates people out of their competencies. To fulfill 19th-century industrial job requirements, we created a hierarchy in education where math and science were at the top and creative thinking was at the bottom. As education began to reward the top-tiered skills like math and science more often, the system became about creating more academics, which in turn undervalued undergraduate degrees. This then caused more and more top-tiered skilled degrees to be created. Not surprisingly, such a system has harmed curiosity and creativity, which are fundamental for innovation.

To better understand this impact, look at the effect it had on children. As part of his work with NASA, Professor George Land created an assessment to test for creativity and studied children to view how their levels changed. He found that at age five, 98% of children were creative geniuses. By age ten, that number fell to 30%. By age 15, that figure dropped to 12%, and by age 31, only 2% were creative geniuses. We need to understand why this occurs.

To help us see where we have created obstacles to creativity and curiosity, let's look at the two kinds of thinking that most people use: divergent and convergent. Simply put, divergent thinking entails using one's imagination to create something new, whereas convergent thinking entails testing and criticizing. Land likens divergent thinking to stepping on a car's accelerator and convergent thinking to stepping on its brake. Step on both at the same time and you do not get far. However, our education system encourages students to do just that. As a result, students come up with new ideas only to then judge and criticize them into non-existence. This is that same perpetual monologue in our mind that almost automatically shuts down any new and potentially valuable ideas we conjure up. Such a voice almost always stops further exploration.

And when we neglect to ask questions and seek insights, our personal lives, jobs, and organizations all suffer. Like a *Mission Impossible* fuse that never gets lit, we exist rather than live. We go about our lives, sometimes in a zombie-like state, failing to engage with the world around us. Far too many of us need more passion for what we do in life. Instead, we look for the next popular thing to stream on television to kill time, and we shout "TGIF!" at the end of every workweek. But what if we could light that match, get that explosion, and blow away a dull world and replace it with one of endless potential?

CHAPTER 3

The Index

The important thing is not to stop questioning. Curiosity has its own reason for existence. One cannot help but be in awe when he contemplates the mysteries of eternity, of life, of the marvelous structure of reality. It is enough if one tries merely to comprehend a little of this mystery each day.

—Albert Einstein

I was about halfway through writing *Cracking the Curiosity Code* when I recognized that we needed to light that *Mission Impossible* match. But how? I found no assessment that uncovered the inhibitors of curiosity, which would be necessary to determining how to improve it. And few studies connected the value of improving curiosity with potential financial gains. I knew that if I wanted to solve the problem, I had to somehow quantify the factors that inhibited it.

Like emotional intelligence, curiosity was a squishy area to describe and measure. I spent years hiring experts and eventually found that even the top statisticians looked at creating the assessment in a status-quo way. They kept coming back with questions that only determined levels of curiosity, which was a wheel I didn't want to reinvent. So, I took my own advice, got out of my comfort zone, and learned how to do all the crazy statistical stuff like factor analysis, which led me to create a valid instrument. I uncovered the four factors that keep people from exploring their natural curiosity, and out of this work the Curiosity Code Index (CCI) was born.

I will examine those four factors in more detail later in the book, but briefly, they include four factors that inhibit curiosity: fear, assumptions, technology, and environment (FATE). Uncovering these four inhibitors of curiosity spurred me to help individuals overcome them to improve their performance at work. This required that I train consultants, HR professionals, and leaders to recognize the impact that their CCI results would have and create actions leading to improvement; it was an enormous task. I wanted to train as many professionals as possible to lead and mentor employees to find more meaning in their jobs and thus make their organizations more productive. But what surprised me the most was not how much work this would take— that seemed obvious. Instead, I was amazed that I needed more correlative data to prove what everyone seems to know intuitively, that curiosity is at the heart of employee engagement as well as just about everything else, like innovation, communication, and ultimately everything that leads to productivity. Even when I asked ChatGPT about the financial connection between curiosity development and productivity, engagement, innovation, etc., it replied that "It's intuitive," and "There's a clear link" with the issue. ChatGPT then provided many examples of how curiosity can improve all those things (productivity, engagement, etc.) but did not tie it down to the bottom line of how much money it was costing organizations. There are limited studies regarding financially based results that stem from improving curiosity.

At this point, I started to collect anecdotal information. Although I found some quantitative data, more is needed, and I hope organizations can perform simple surveys and follow-ups after providing curiosity training to generate this data. Some, like Novartis, have. They measured curiosity and engagement levels, provided a culture of curiosity training, and then measured both again. As of this writing, they have yet to publish this data publicly, but they have moved the needle. Imagine the financial impact of improving engagement! Based on Gallup's findings, we currently lose more than $550 billion a year due to low engagement. If we could tie curiosity to engagement and then find a way to enhance it, that might be the first step in increasing engagement and reaping its attendant financial benefits.

Again, data that supports a link between engagement and curiosity is often not published, which makes it impossible for the Internet and AI to find it. This happens because organizations share their results internally. I enjoy working with leaders who want to undertake research like that carried out by Novartis. But in reality, many leaders do not need hard data; instead, they see this issue the way AI does, as intuitive.

What is frustrating is that even though these leaders know that curiosity is essential and affects their bottom line, developing curiosity so that their employees will be happier requires a culture change. Many organizations are stuck in the past. It is easier to keep doing what has always worked than to start doing something new. However, that is the mistake that Kodak and Blockbuster made. Unfortunately for such organizations, the world continues to evolve and old ways no longer address new problems.

Think of the organizations that have used foresight and innovative thinking to be successful. Take Domino's, for example. Their innovation began when they launched a mobile ordering system; it now generates more than 80% of their sales. Their tracker and pizza builder features allow customers to see their pizza being built on their screen. So, what did quitting status-quo behaviors do for their bottom line? Well, in 2010 when they launched their turnaround and began to innovate, their stock price was $9 a share; as of this writing, it is more than $400.

Becoming a Domino's and not a Blockbuster requires embracing innovative thinking and abandoning status-quo thinking. And the first step to abandoning the past is to recognize what holds you back and to build a plan to overcome it. And that is what this book will teach you.

Here, you will learn about organizations that have managed to abandon status-quo thinking and its negative impact. You will also discover how curiosity ties into organizational challenges like increasing engagement, developing innovation and sound leadership, and fostering good communication, emotional intelligence, and motivation—all of which lead to productivity. Additionally, you will read about products that were born out of curiosity, AI's impact on curiosity, stories of those who used curiosity to succeed, and how curiosity can help you at work and at home. Most importantly, you will learn much of what I have taught worldwide in my training programs. This critical knowledge will help you find what inhibits your curiosity and formulate a plan to overcome those issues.

But to do all this you must first put aside your fear and your assumptions (aka the voices in your head) and recognize that you might over- or under-utilize technology as you uncover how others may have impacted your own natural curiosity. If you do that and follow the principles in this book, you will learn how to explore interests you didn't even know you had. And as you do that, you will find more joy in your job. And as you lead, you will learn how to create the kind of work culture that inspired this book.

Let's begin your journey by exploring the financial impact that curiosity can have at work, including its costs and potential gains. Because if you want to build a better organization and a better you, you need to learn how to harness curiosity.

PART II

FINANCIAL
IMPLICATIONS

Every year, organizations lose money because of poor communication, low employee motivation, and weak employee engagement, among other issues. But when we recognize that fostering a culture of curiosity enables employees to engage better as they explore opportunities within their roles, we can see the critical link between curiosity and all of the above challenges. Individuals fueled by curiosity are not just passive participants in their work; they become actively engaged and inspired to ask questions, seek knowledge, and contribute meaningfully to their workplace culture. Fostering curiosity is no longer a choice but a strategic imperative for organizations seeking to create a culture that not only fuels innovation but also tackles challenges posed by cutting-edge technologies like AI. In this way, a curious workforce sees and embraces technology as an enabler of human ingenuity, not as a threat.

And as employees explore their options, this helps them align better with organizational objectives, thereby significantly improving engagement levels. Leaders must grasp the tangible connection between curiosity and the organization's bottom line, a correlation that extends far beyond mere academic understanding.

Effective leadership is not just about making decisions and issuing directives. Truly influential leaders understand the transformative power of curiosity and actively emulate the organizational culture they desire. They do this by asking questions, fostering an environment where individuals feel encouraged to provide insights and even fail—recognizing failure as a way to learn critical lessons and continue to improve.

When leaders foster curiosity, communication, which is often viewed as a soft skill, takes center stage. To communicate openly and effectively, individuals must listen actively. This not only improves empathy and emotional intelligence but also breaks down silos within the organization. Open communication promotes collaboration and allows us to better understand diverse perspectives, thereby limiting the biases that hinder teamwork.

When individuals feel accepted and rewarded for their insights, motivation and productivity increase. A workplace culture that values curiosity and encourages open communication creates an environment that motivates its members to contribute and find satisfaction in their work.

In essence, the connection between curiosity and the multifaceted challenges leaders face is not just theoretical; it's a tangible reality that organizations can harness to achieve sustainable success. Leaders simply need to begin viewing curiosity as both a desirable quality and an essential force that generates organizational success.

CHAPTER 4

Engagement and Alignment

If you can let go of passion, and follow your curiosity,
your curiosity might just lead you to your passion.

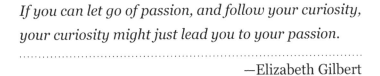

—Elizabeth Gilbert

As previously stated, Gallup found that in the U.S., organizations lose $550 billion a year because of low engagement. They also estimated that this costs the global economy some $7.8 trillion. We know that less than a third of workers feel engaged at work. But what does that mean? Gallup defines engaged employees as "those who are involved in, enthusiastic about, and committed to their work and workplace." Employees who feel aligned with their passions are more likely to contribute to the organization's success.

Engagement often comes up as a topic in the graduate classes I teach. And these courses often include an excellent case study about how Doug Conant improved engagement at Campbell's Soup. I've been fortunate to interview Doug multiple times and I asked him how he managed to take his employees' engagement from 62% not actively engaged and 12% actively disengaged to

67% actively engaged. This change is far above the change that Gallup labels as world-class. Conant's actions, and the resulting change, helped his company outperform the S&P Food Group and the S&P 500.

To improve engagement, Conant utilized curiosity. He shared with me that he asked questions about the workplace culture and created the "Campbell Promise," which was "Campbell valuing people, people valuing Campbell." But just creating a slogan or motto does nothing if their words are not implemented.

To do that, Conant developed an annual survey to measure his company's ability to improve his employees' trust. He then used information from the survey to celebrate successes. Conant is known for giving his employees thank-you notes—around 20 a day for years—and for providing group lunches to seek out employee perspectives on problems. I asked him how many thank-you notes he's written over the years, and he estimated it was around 30,000. Doing this seems so simple—and yet so few do it. Doug is one of the humblest leaders I have ever met, and it was clear that he was willing to learn from others. His actions not only improved his company's financial and market performance, but they revitalized the culture and made it more innovative, even during a difficult economy.

The questions Doug Conant asked in his surveys that led to his thank-you notes required him to create a culture of curiosity, a culture that rewarded the gathering of information. When leaders embrace and encourage curiosity, they can shift their organization's culture. Unfortunately, many leaders believe they do this, but their employees do not share their belief. There is often a disconnect between what leaders assume will motivate their employees and what actually motivates them.

I once worked as a mortgage sales professional. As in many sales organizations, we were offered many so-called perks to improve our performance. The two I remember most were tickets to a Phoenix Suns basketball game and dinner at a fine restaurant. On the surface, those sound like good incentives. However, as I did not enjoy going out at night, these perks would be more of a burden than a reward. In the end, they never offered me an incentive that would have worked. Why? Because no one ever asked. Had they asked, I might have told them that I preferred going home an hour earlier (to spend time with my kids). As well-intentioned as they were, those incentives were based on false assumptions. Again, to find the right incentives for me, all the management had to do was ask. It would have been so simple.

Sometimes, organizations ask questions through surveys. For surveys to work, however, the organization needs to share the results. When I worked as a sales representative for one of the world's largest organizations, I remember taking an annual survey asking about my job and how the organization did things. After 15 years of taking that survey, I don't recall ever being told the results or what changes had been made because of those surveys. For surveys to work, people need to hear that their input matters. Even if something as simple as a coffee machine has been added as a result of input from a survey, employees need to hear about it so they will know that their answers and opinions matter.

For people to feel engaged, they must be passionate about what they do. But how do we determine their passions in organizations that do not actively promote curiosity? That has been the challenge. Leaders often make (sometimes false) assumptions about what people enjoy or should enjoy doing.

When I was working in pharmaceutical sales, I remember one meeting where management seated us around a large, round table and asked us what we liked most and least about our jobs. The person to my left started by sharing that she enjoyed driving her car. As everyone followed going clockwise, I noticed most shared the same thing; driving was a big part of what they found relaxing and rewarding. I was stunned. When my turn finally came, I shared that I liked doing paperwork and working at the computer, but that driving was absolutely the worst part of my day. Oddly enough, what I actually liked doing happened to be what everyone else at that table had said was the *worst* part of their job.

Clearly, I did not feel very engaged being a pharmaceutical rep. When I started at that company just out of high school, I had worked as a secretary and loved it. During that roundtable, I realized that I had loved my job then because my position was administrative. This was a light bulb moment for me. When I eventually left that organization, I looked for the most paperwork-laden job I could find. That led to my career in lending, where I was much better aligned and experienced much better engagement.

Now I'm sure many of you reading this can't imagine why anyone would prefer paperwork to driving! But that is what's wonderful about people; we are all unique. If everyone liked doing the same things, it would be challenging to fill every job. But since we are so different, we must embrace those differences. When leaders assume that all their employees love to drive and hate to do paperwork, some of their employees will end up improperly aligned. I might still be working for that organization had there been a more administrative position in that division. Instead, I stayed in a job I disliked for 15 years and was sad every Sunday night because I knew I had to return to that job the next day. Once I left that job, however, I again looked forward to Mondays.

What if our employees don't like any of the tasks their job requires? That can happen. The good news is that there is probably a job somewhere that they do like. They need only experience the same aha! moment I did to help them switch to a different position, division, or organization. This problem can often be alleviated by assigning employees to different responsibilities than traditionally provided in that job. But if no internal solutions can be found and an employee who is not engaged leaves the company, their departure is a win-win for both the organization and that individual.

* * *

Organizations often administer engagement surveys because they recognize their importance. However, follow-up can sometimes prove challenging. It requires leadership commitment, organizational culture change, sources to support and analyze results, communication, and action planning. Typically, companies keep internal feedback and engagement survey results confidential. However, engagement survey follow-up varies widely by organization, and only some share their results publicly. For engagement surveys to work, organizations should prioritize transparency and communication and internally share information about their initiatives.

To improve employee engagement, leaders should ask a mix of strategic and open-ended questions that encourage honest feedback, identify areas for improvement, and demonstrate a genuine interest in the well-being of their team.

Here are some questions that leaders can ask:

- How satisfied are you with your current role and responsibilities?
- On a scale of 1 to 10, how fulfilled do you feel in your work?
- (To receive feedback on leadership) What are the strengths of our current leadership team? How can leadership better support you in your role?
- (Regarding communication and transparency) How would you rate communication within the team/organization? Are you kept well-informed about important decisions and changes?
- (For professional development) Are there opportunities for career growth and development here? How can the organization better support your professional goals?
- (Regarding work-life balance) How would you describe your current work-life balance? What changes could improve it?

- (To determine proper recognition and appreciation) Do you feel recognized and appreciated for your contributions? Are there particular achievements or efforts you believe deserve acknowledgment?
- (For team dynamics) How would you describe the team dynamics within your department? Are there ways we can enhance collaboration and teamwork?
- (Regarding feedback on processes and systems) Are there any processes or systems that hinder your productivity? How can we improve existing workflows or tools to make your job easier?
- (To determine general job satisfaction) What aspects of your job do you find most satisfying? Are there elements of your role that you find challenging or unfulfilling?
- (For well-being and support) How would you rate the level of support you receive for your well-being? Are there specific resources or initiatives that could enhance your overall well-being?
- (For diversity and inclusion) How do you perceive the organization's commitment to diversity and inclusion? Are there ways we can foster a more inclusive work environment?
- (To determine employee engagement initiatives) Have you found value in any recent employee engagement initiatives? What additional activities or programs would you like to see to enhance team morale?

These questions should explore most aspects of the employee experience. For surveys to be effective and foster a positive and engaging work environment, leaders must actively listen, respond to feedback, and act based on the information gathered.

CHAPTER 5

AI and Innovation

The path to innovation begins with curiosity.

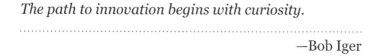

—Bob Iger

One of the most critical things an organization can do today is to remain innovative. With artificial intelligence changing the workplace landscape, employees who are proactive and have foresight will have the edge. Because I serve on multiple boards of advisors, including those of AI-based organizations, I have witnessed first-hand many of the challenges AI can resolve and (potentially) cause. The leaders who understand these challenges will create a culture that embraces curiosity, which in turn leads to innovation.

One of the most recent AI elements to make headlines is ChatGPT. To test it out, I questioned it to see what it knew about the financial value of improving curiosity as well as curiosity's relationship to innovation. I asked, "What research do you have to support that developing curiosity is critical to improving innovation in the workplace and the financial benefits it provides?" Its response:

As of my last knowledge update in January 2022, substantial research and literature support the idea that developing curiosity is critical for fostering innovation in the workplace, and there are associated financial benefits. While direct financial impact may be challenging to quantify precisely, increased innovation and employee engagement are often linked to improved financial performance. Innovations can lead to developing new products or services, improved processes, and a competitive edge in the market.

Although this is good news, the problem is that ChatGPT lists no research or data to back up these statements, making this "substantial research" difficult to find. Another reason this data is difficult to find is that many organizations do not publish their internal findings—though I wish they would. In short, ChatGPT is telling us that these findings are intuitive and obvious.

ChatGPT included additional insight into how engagement ties into creativity and referenced an *HBR* article that does not give financial numbers. The problem is that no matter how I asked for bottom-line financial numbers, ChatGPT kept responding that the process was intuitive. I believe this is because there is little research available. I have worked with organizations that have tied curiosity to engagement and found that doing so produced a positive financial outcome, but I want more organizations to focus on creating and publishing critical data on this subject so that AI can share it with the world.

It's challenging to rely on ChatGPT or other forms of AI to provide data that does not exist. Computers are only as good as the information we provide them with. A *Wall Street Journal* article stated that Elon Musk was one of the founders of ChatGPT but left when he believed the software might have been influenced by political ideology. If Musk, or someone like him, creates their own AI platform, what's stopping them from influencing it with their own political ideology?

That is why developing curiosity is so critical. One of the factors that the Curiosity Code Index discovered impacted curiosity was the under- and over-utilization of technology. I conducted my research before ChatGPT and software like it became popular. Since then, more technology exists that is likely to impact curiosity.

Consider the value of using AI technology and curiosity to evaluate research results. Over the thousands of business classes I have taught, I often hear from other instructors who worry that students will now use AI to do their homework and write their term papers for them. While institutions are aware of this problem, discerning between student-generated work and AI-generated work is often challenging. Thanks to the rise of plagiarism detectors and other methods, educators are now a little better equipped to distinguish when a student has used AI to do their work.

While testing ChatGPT's capabilities, I used it to see if I could write an entire graduate-level course, as well as an entire book about curiosity. And I did this in hours. That is astounding, and you might wonder if I used ChatGPT to create this current book. While I do use AI to do research at times, AI does not yet have the knowledge I have and therefore cannot share my stories. However, I think that AI software can help improve original work. To me, using AI is similar to using a platform like Grammarly to edit one's writing and make it more compelling. Grammarly and similar platforms have been available for many years, and as they improve they receive more attention.

So, how do we improve our curiosity and, as a result, our critical thinking skills to better utilize AI? That is a vital question. If we under- or over-utilize technology, we must recognize that we are missing out on developing our curiosity.

Many feel that learning technology is unnecessary or that it requires too much complex information to understand. Often, such people simply need to become aware of its possibilities and uses to appreciate its importance. It is common to hear older adults rage against or even reject new technology. But many younger adults also feel challenged by it. As technology keeps changing, one can become overwhelmed and feel that learning and keeping up with its advancements requires too much time and energy. When people experience this information overload, they often have no idea where to start in order to learn about technology. Almost everyone, it seems, ends up facing these issues.

As leaders, we must give our people a solid foundation in technology. We must allow them to ask questions and not let them get overwhelmed by it. Consider the calculator. What if none of us had ever learned the math behind it? Worse yet, what if someone had given Einstein a calculator (had it existed then) but never taught him the math behind it? He might have become the most excellent calculator operator in the world, but he would never have become the genius he was. We must first gain a foundational understanding of technology and then learn how best to use it. Of course, to effectively put all this into practice requires curiosity.

Again, one area of technology we need to learn is AI-powered software like ChatGPT. Learning what it can do requires that we be curious enough to ask questions. Learning how accurate it is requires that we think critically and research the sources it provides. Naturally, as AI becomes more sophisticated, individuals and organizations will find more uses for it.

Consider an organization like RadiusAI, which uses AI to help convenience stores decrease shrinkage (i.e., losses due to shoplifting, cashier error, employee theft, etc.). The stores had a problem—shrinkage—and that problem drove the software makers to be curious about how AI could possibly solve it. As a result, RadiusAI created software that could identify when customers put two slices of pizza into a box instead of one or fill their cup with expensive Red Bull instead of a less expensive soda before purchasing it. Curiosity about the massive losses due to theft in convenience stores not only sparked RadiusAI to pursue a solution, it also helped them engineer that solution. In that way, curiosity helped create an innovation that can save retail organizations millions of dollars.

AI is only effective if we utilize our curiosity to shape AI to make it more curious. AI can determine security threats, investigate incidents, solve problems, and much more. However, AI relies on us to input what we want it to uncover. AI has adaptive learning capabilities, meaning that it can adjust its output based on what it discovers. And rather than relying on intrinsic rewards (i.e., the psychological rewards we get from doing something well, which AI can't experience), AI tries to reduce uncertainty.

But how curious do we want to allow AI to be? Elon Musk has said that he wants to build a safe AI system: "From an AI safety standpoint ... a maximally curious AI, one that is trying to understand the universe, is, I think, going to be pro-humanity." In other words, not everyone (including Musk) thinks that AI will automatically be safe or put human needs and interests first. Thus, this debate over AI and its potential for harm needs to happen because no one wants us to lose control and have AI take over.

Despite some dire warnings about AI and its potential for harm, AI and the technology that drives it continue to develop. Consider the role curiosity plays in ambient computing. Ambient computing refers to technology seamlessly integrated into our environment, with devices communicating and collaborating via a natural interface, such as voice commands, facial recognition, gesture recognition, proximity sensors, etc. Curiosity can develop those systems by understanding preferences and environmental cues. To create natural interactive interfaces, designers must be curious about how our gestures might impact them, how to make them more novel, and how to personalize them.

But how are organizations utilizing curiosity and AI going to increase innovation?

Consider Amazon and the questions it asks customers so it can improve product recommendations, make their supply chain more efficient, and determine future demand and inventory (to route orders efficiently). Asking the right questions requires thought and analysis as well as software programs that use AI to analyze images and videos. Without curiosity, which spurs the desire to ask the right questions, Amazon would lose many opportunities to improve its business and its logistics.

Organizations like Starbucks have used AI to determine the most competitive locations and traffic patterns and to conduct revenue forecasting. I met with McDonald's leaders when they launched their curiosity-based program globally. They use generative AI to innovate and reduce restaurant crew complexity. Coca-Cola used AI to help its research staff create Coca-Cola's Y3000 Zero Sugar. They also used AI to determine how their customers envision the future of flavors, colors, and more.

Not to be outdone, PepsiCo used AI to analyze millions of social media posts, gathering information for less than a year, to help it develop new snacks. Not surprisingly, Uber uses AI to design self-driving vehicles and automated street sign detections for map-building that can increase these cars' navigation accuracy and lead to more efficient routing, among other benefits. Target even uses AI to predict if a person is pregnant before they know it themselves! AI is ubiquitous, whether it helps us open our iPhone with our face or ask Alexa to play our favorite song. Facebook's AI software can recognize your face better than humans can, making it able to quickly detect and remove harmful images.

These are just a few examples of organizations that understand how curiosity leads to innovation. At the same time, many organizations cling to past status-quo successes, which is the biggest killer of innovation. To stay on the cutting edge, be relevant, and create an organization that succeeds, we must use our curiosity to take advantage of AI and other technologies.

To best use AI, we need curious individuals to ask the right questions. They must research, design, train, and input ethical considerations as they use feedback to improve, monitor, and ensure that different disciplines collaborate with each other. To improve collaboration, counter bias, and improve our education system, we must ensure that there are no cultural barriers.

Organizations that fail to use curiosity to tap into the value of AI will likely suffer from inefficiencies, missed productivity gains, increased labor costs, and reduced data analytics and insights. They might also undergo diminished customer experience, misallocation of resources, security risks, a lack of scalability, and compliance difficulties. In short, organizations that reject curiosity and AI in favor of status-quo ways of doing and thinking will likely bear these costs—and a great many more.

Improving technology will impact existing jobs while also creating new ones. And the faster technology improves, the faster these impacts will occur. When I worked for a value-added reseller selling IBM System 36s and 38s in the mid-1980s, similar concerns about job loss and a computer takeover existed even then. At that time, we could never have imagined a position like 'social media manager' because social media had yet to exist.

We must utilize our curiosity to develop positions that leverage technology's new capabilities to expand our own. But first, we must expand our curiosity by recognizing what inhibits it and create programs and plans to prevent this inhibition. If we do so, we will harness the best of technology, like AI, while also using and treasuring those human qualities that AI cannot possess in order to reach newer, greater heights.

CHAPTER 6

Leadership

Successful leaders are curious about others and learning how others do things so that they, the leaders, can learn and become better versions of themselves.

—Allegra van Hövell-Patrizi

I am often asked during my speaking engagements how best to ask questions or allow curiosity when leaders do not embrace it. The *Harvard Business Review*'s (*HBR*) Business Case for Curiosity found that leaders *say* they value inquisitive minds. And yet, most leaders continue to stifle curiosity. Why? Most likely because they fear it will increase risk and inefficiency. However, leaders who focus too much on efficiency can undermine long-term results. *HBR* reported that 25% of employees felt curious about their jobs, while 70% faced barriers to asking questions.

Based on my experience, individuals eager to pose questions to leaders often worry that their inquiries might be perceived as confrontational or as doubting the leader's expertise. And they are not wrong to feel that way. Most leaders have moments when they wonder if they are qualified to do their job. This is called the imposter syndrome.

It is not uncommon to run into leaders who feel threatened by employees who might have more knowledge or experience. When considering how people react, sometimes it's not how a company is set up but its culture that inhibits curiosity and sets a negative tone. I once worked for a company whose headquarters was a huge building where all the big bosses had their offices up on the top floor. Nobody else was even allowed to go up there. I remember one time when my boss invited me to a board meeting on that exclusive floor. I had to fly in from Arizona just for that meeting. It was my very first time being allowed up there and I have to admit; I was curious.

When I got off the elevator, which needed a special key just to open on that floor, I saw glass doors that kept the top bosses separated from everyone else. One of the leaders wasn't happy about me being there for a meeting she wasn't invited to, so she actually stopped me right at those glass doors. Despite my having been invited and flying in especially to attend, she didn't even allow me past those doors. She would rather have the company spend time and money to fly me there and do nothing than allow me on that floor.

That company's leaders never came down to see the rest of us work and even had someone make sure I couldn't get through even when I was invited and was right there at the door. This really sent a message about the culture of the organization; the big bosses didn't mix with the rest of us workers. And had they had a different corporate structure, it wouldn't have mattered; their culture was, in a word, negative.

Leaders are simply people, and people naturally have insecurities. No one can know everything, which is why leaders who admit that they don't know everything, and who surround themselves with advisors and mentors who excel in areas that they do not, have often inspired me. For leaders to overcome the imposter syndrome, they must learn to trust others and admit they do not and cannot have all the answers.

But what if your leader has yet to realize that? If so, then the best way to ask them a question is to buffer it. Consider how a leader might react to the following two questions: If I were to ask, "Why do we have to do it that way?" how would their reaction differ from being asked, "I want to be sure I understand. I am trying to develop my curiosity, so I hope you don't mind if I ask you a question. Would you mind explaining the outcomes we hope to achieve by changing how we do that?" Both questions seek the same information, but the second presents the employee as more humble (versus an almost lazy or even confrontational attitude in the first question) because that employee admits that they themselves do not have the answer. Moreover, the second question is kinder because it doesn't put the leader on the defensive.

If leaders need a reason to curb imposter syndrome, it is that this syndrome inhibits the curiosity of both leaders and their employees. It can be challenging, but we must admit that everyone makes mistakes. Denying this fact leads to status-quo thinking, which kills innovation. You might have heard the expressions 'to fail often' or 'to fail forward'. Some organizations, like Google, understand the value of failing forward, and they urge their people to take chances. Humble leaders who share their own failures are more likely to get the people they lead to take more risks.

I have met great leaders who surround themselves with top thinkers who share their knowledge and enhance their ability to lead. Keith Krach is one such leader. I chose him to write the foreword to *Cracking the Curiosity Code* because I witnessed how effective he was at developing curiosity in others and in himself. I was fortunate to serve as a member of his board of advisor group when he was CEO and Chairman at DocuSign. I was inspired by how he connected with some of the world's most brilliant, influential leaders and how he knew that he could learn from all of them. I was humbled that he included me in such a group. Keith saw things in people that others did not. He saw that we could all complement each other's abilities and knowledge. When we form advisory groups like that, everyone in them wins.

I have served on many other organizations' boards and learned something from each of them. Leaders should also have a personal board of advisors or mentors from whom they can gain knowledge. I would never want to be the most intelligent person in a room—that would be very boring. When we surround ourselves with those who know things we don't, the impact is tremendous. Such mentors can often share what did and did not work for them, which can help us avoid reinventing the wheel. And as we learn how to share our failures and our lessons learned, we can learn to overcome our fear of being perfect. If we recognize the value of mentorship, we can promote it to those who work for us.

When our employees find mentors, they can learn self-confidence, avoid bias, and improve cultural awareness. That requires leaders to look at how they can improve their organizations.

Leaders must ask questions about what their employees need and reflect on what holds them back personally.

Unfortunately, many organizations do not offer much leadership training. When I worked in education, I was stunned by the scarcity of leadership education. Although I was trained to find reports and job descriptions, I was not trained to be a leader. Many organizations justify their lack of leadership training because of its high cost. Instead, they should calculate the even higher opportunity cost of *not* providing training.

Reinventing the wheel wastes everyone's time and costs a lot. Instead of having multiple Zoom meetings about upcoming Zoom meetings, organizations could better spend that time uncovering best practices on how to do the job and then training everyone on how to be more efficient and effective. We need to be curious about what has slipped through the cracks and what we need to do to improve.

Thinking outside the box is what it takes to thrive in today's environment, which is why leaders must understand how to find new ways to train and develop curiosity. Leaders must ask questions about what does and does not work in their organizations. They must allow input and must question status-quo behavior. And this may require them to change their culture in order to improve communication and develop curiosity.

In 2022, I was part of a panel for the Forbes School of Business and Technology's Thought Leader Summit, hosted by Dr. Katie Thiry, where we discussed the flattening of organizations. This topic continues to be challenging for organizations due to the pros and cons of having a hierarchical structure versus a flatter one. Many organizations continue to explore and implement flatter structures to foster greater agility, innovation, and employee empowerment. Curiosity plays a critical role in that exploration.

When I interviewed top CHROs for the Global Mentor Network, we touched on some fascinating trends about companies where they worked on structure and cultural changes. I obtained insights from leaders at Cardinal Health, DocuSign, Juniper, Comerica, Encore Capital, MetLife, Rent the Runway, and others.

One recurring topic was this idea of dual leadership; having two people share one management role. It's like having a mentor and a hands-on manager rolled into one team. This arrangement might remind you of that episode from *The Office* where Michael and Jim are co-managers, which at the time seemed pretty crazy. And yet today we have real-world examples where this model has actually been successful.

Take Warby Parker, for instance. The eyewear company has two CEOs, Neil Blumenthal and Dave Gilboa, who've been sharing the top spot since the company started. They've managed to make Warby Parker into a billion-dollar brand, proving that two heads in the same role can be better than one. Another example is Whole Foods, which had co-CEOs John Mackey and

Walter Robb. Under their dual leadership, Whole Foods grew significantly and maintained its position as a leader in organic groceries.

Curiosity plays an important part in designing an organization's structure so that it meets current needs and also adapts to future challenges. By not relying on past status-quo ways, Warby Parker and Whole Foods have achieved significant growth and success.

Some organizations have transitioned to flatter structures and experienced agility, innovation, and improvements in engagement. Google has focused on a more team-oriented and flexible structure. Their cross-functional teams and open workplace have led to many successful innovations. Spotify organizes employees into autonomous squads, creating a culture of creativity and quick adaptation to change. Zappos implemented a "Holacracy" to distribute authority throughout the organization, which improved engagement and creativity. However, Zappos faced some issues. As some employees found the new alignment confusing, in 2020 they reverted to the more traditional structure. Zappos is one of many organizations that found the transition did not work well for them, while Cisco, IBM, Microsoft, Morning Star, Walmart, and many others found that some structure adaptations (i.e., making their organization flatter) had to be reconsidered.

On the other hand, many organizations have successfully transitioned to a flatter structure by asking how to make it work. The success of such changes can depend on how healthy organizations utilize curiosity to be proactive and have foresight about the implications of that decision. They must also ask the question (as Zappos did) about whether their experimental change was successful. No decision can be made in a vacuum, and as plans change, so do decisions. Which is why organizations must have a curiosity-based culture that does not rely on the status quo.

Sometimes, it takes a major event to get people out of status-quo thinking. COVID-19 shook up the way organizations thought about the future of work. Organizations (and their people) began to emphasize remote work, employee well-being, diversity and inclusion, agile and adaptive learning, remote team building and socialization, purpose-driven initiatives, and flexible work arrangements. The pandemic made organizations recognize that the power of the employee had grown. Employees began to expect more; they got used to working from home and that changed their idea of work/life balance.

To adapt to the new work culture, organizations utilized curiosity to encourage employees to explore and embrace tools that improved collaboration. They emphasized the value of flexibility in work arrangements to make life more meaningful for their employees. They also required employees to adopt digital tools and improve their problem-solving skills. As teams collaborated virtually, curiosity helped foster a sense of community to learn more ways to connect.

The successful organizations ensured curiosity played an essential role in their post-COVID strategies by encouraging questions and rewarding curiosity-driven behaviors. They created learning opportunities, promoted cross-functional collaboration, explored new technologies, emphasized problem-solving and critical thinking skills, encouraged inclusive decision-making, and promoted leaders who had a learning-oriented mindset.

Organizations also adopted crisis preparedness planning. A successful plan requires curiosity by encouraging scenario exploration. What if a potential crisis occurred? What were their plans for such a scenario? Organizations asked questions about failure points and areas of vulnerability to address and identify risks and weaknesses. Going forward, organizations must adopt new technologies, develop crisis simulation exercises, establish communication channels, and adopt a curious mindset that gathers external perspectives.

Organizations that have yet to recognize the importance of developing a curiosity-based culture can experience multiple issues with crisis-preparedness. Should a crisis occur, their limited problem-solving skills, missed opportunities, and inefficient resources will put them up against the wall. Additionally, their inability to embrace a curiosity-based culture reveals a more risk-averse organization, a mind-set that could slow innovation and deter growth following a crisis.

Over the past several years, organizations have experienced much change, some of it due to the pandemic, some of it due to technological growth and societal change. These changes have included a move toward remote work, economic uncertainty, supply chain disruptions, difficulty finding and retaining talent, cybersecurity threats, and increased concern over the mental health and well-being of employees. Organizations have had to deal with environmental social and governance (ESG) priorities, which have become politically controversial. These topics include anti-competition, business ethics, intellectual property, tax fraud privacy, environmental issues, and diversity, opportunity, and inclusion (DEI). They also have had to deal with global geopolitical tensions, regulatory changes, and continuity planning.

Some organizations have begun to address these issues using a curiosity-based approach. One such company is Pfizer. Their collaboration with BioNTech helped develop the first COVID-19 vaccine and helped Pfizer reap $100 billion in earnings in 2022, as it showcased Pfizer's ability to innovate. In another instance, Microsoft's collaboration tools helped organizations transition to remote work and improved their overall revenue. Amazon has constantly evaluated and adapted its business model, which has helped it create diverse revenue streams. Apple diversifies its suppliers to address and prevent supply chain challenges, which makes Apple more resilient and has helped them reap record profits. Salesforce's cloud-based service expansion and investment in artificial intelligence have contributed to its economic success. And companies like Palo Alto Networks have thwarted cybersecurity threats because they actively explore new technologies.

Leaders have never had as much on their plate as they do now. And although this can be overwhelming and lead to information overload, curiosity can help make their jobs easier. Leaders who are curious are more inclined to seek new information, stay abreast of industry trends, and embrace emerging technologies. The ongoing pursuit of knowledge helps them navigate complex challenges and make informed decisions, ultimately streamlining their decision-making processes. By exploring alternative approaches and challenging the status quo, leaders can uncover innovative strategies that simplify their tasks and propel their organization forward. This adaptive problem-solving approach makes their jobs easier and positions them to address challenges with greater efficiency and effectiveness.

Additionally, an inclusive communication style builds stronger relationships, promotes collaboration, and helps leaders stay attuned to their team's needs, which in turn creates a more cohesive and harmonious work environment. Lastly, curiosity builds resilience because leaders who approach challenges with curiosity are better equipped to adapt to change and uncertainty. Rather than be overwhelmed by information, curious leaders view change as an opportunity for growth, learning, and improvement.

CHAPTER 7

Communication

The greatest problem with communication is we don't listen to understand. We listen to reply. When we listen with curiosity, we don't listen with the intent to reply. We listen for what's behind the words.

—Stephen Covey

Although organizations can experience significant financial losses due to poor communication and conflict, this trend can be reversed by fostering curiosity. Alas, organizations sometimes inadvertently train their people to be less curious.

When I was a pharmaceutical representative, my company put us through intensive communication training, some of the best I've ever received. They taught us that delivering our message clearly to doctors was important. They drilled it into our heads that we needed to say certain things in a certain way to ensure that others received our message correctly. They were so strict with how we should communicate that they videotaped our sales presentations. They called giving vital information to our doctors, "detailing the doctors." As a result, we had to watch our "detail" recordings and ensure that every word we said was correct. I witnessed managers belittle my coworkers who did not do this properly.

I was so stressed about saying the correct thing that I practiced for hours and hours every week. I remember the first time I went to present to a busy physician. As I sat in the waiting room, mulling over everything I needed to say, I worried most about getting to discuss all three of my products. We had been told that doctors usually had no time and would probably walk away while we tried to sell them. So, I was prepared for that.

I was pleasantly surprised when this first doctor allowed me to sit in his office, across from him at his desk, and give my detail presentation. I can remember going through all three products. I couldn't believe my luck! I was so proud of myself. I walked out of that office on a cloud, patting myself on the back all the way to the elevator. I had to go downstairs to get samples for him. A man joined me in the elevator and, as it descended a few floors, I found it hard, as an extravert, to endure the awkward silence. So, I asked him if he worked in the building.

He looked at me and told me that *he* was the doctor I had just given the detailed presentation to! I was mortified. It was then that I realized that I had not even looked at him, much less asked him any questions, during my entire sales call. What I believed had been the best presentation was actually the worst. I had not found out his pain points, gathered any input to tailor my talk or involved him in any way. I often think about how long I might have continued to present in that way had he not walked onto that elevator with me. Who is not getting on the elevator with you to tell you that you need to communicate more effectively?

Although my organization taught me what to say, they also needed to teach me how to communicate effectively. I remember talking to my boss about this experience, and he told me to forget everything they'd taught me and just speak to the doctor in a conversational way. One day he rode along with me and I watched as he analyzed the room to see where the doctor had gone to school or how many kids were in his photographs. He tailored what he said based on what he saw. It was a life-changing moment for me.

Thanks to that experience, I learned the value of asking questions and of empathy. And that led to my interest in perception. Sometimes, we don't know what we don't know until someone tells us that a big piece of the puzzle is missing. Communication is tricky, and sometimes we don't even hear what we think we hear when we ask questions.

Consider the old game called 'telephone'. You whisper something into someone's ear and they whisper what they heard into the next person's ear, and it goes around a circle until, finally, it reaches the last person who says what they heard. The message always differs from the one originally whispered. Sometimes, it is so dramatically different as to be unrecognizable. Unfortunately, that is often how communication works in the modern workplace.

Perception can also impair our ability to understand a message. In our book *The Power of Perception*, my co-author Dr. Maja Zelihic and I wrote about the impact of perception on communication. We explained that an EPIC process impacts perception, where EPIC stands for how we evaluate, predict, interpret, and correlate to arrive at conclusions. Our IQ, EQ, CQ (cultural quotient), and CQ (curiosity quotient) all influence those steps.

We each view things from slightly different perspectives and vantage points. If we do not ask questions and delve into the meaning behind communication, we fill in the gaps of what we assume was meant based on our background, culture, and what we believe to be true.

I can't tell you how often people have reached out to me, since they know I wrote my dissertation on emotional intelligence, to ask me to read something and give my opinion. Sometimes, they read me an email and ask if I think it sounds snarky; they often read it to me in a sarcastic tone. As I don't know the author, I detect no snarky tone. Sometimes, I read it back to them in a pleasant voice to gauge their reaction. But they often seem confused and even annoyed when I do that because they had wanted to hear that snarky tone!

While the person who wrote the email could have intended it to be snarky, I would need to have had some experience of them to know for sure. However, don't we owe it to one another to listen and read objectively and not make assumptions? Isn't it better to take the high road and give people the benefit of the doubt? When we do not and instead respond with snark, we pour fuel onto the fire. We're only human; sometimes our ego gets in the way of us taking the high road.

Forbes magazine reported that forty-two percent of workers experience stress trying to form responses that convey the right tone of voice. I consider communication style so critical that one of my entry-level business courses was heavily focused on it. My students quickly learned that WRITING IN ALL CAPS denotes yelling as we taught them netiquette (online etiquette) in a distance-based education atmosphere.

But how do we get over past experiences with people who have left a bitter taste? The answer is to speak with them and ask questions about why there were issues in the past. We must address the elephant in the room. The Society for Human Resource Management (SHRM) reported that David Grossman's research, titled "The Cost of Poor Communications," which surveyed 400 companies with 100,000 employees, found that each company cited an average loss of $62.4 million per year because of inadequate communication with and between employees. Miscommunication has even been estimated to cost smaller companies (100 employees or fewer) an average of $420,000 annually.

A State of the Workplace article in *Forbes* reported communication issues from a 2023 study. Workers spend an average of 20 hours a week using digital communications, so how we interpret that information is critical. While digital communication allows more people to feel connected, they also believe they have to be more available, which has led to burnout and, as a result, low productivity.

One of my favorite YouTube videos, Tripp and Tyler's "A Conference Call in Real Life," illustrates the frustrations of communicating during audio conference calls (speaking while on 'mute' or hearing a dog bark or many other issues). The video shows how challenging it can be to communicate effectively on a conference call. When co-creator Tripp Crosby was on my show, he talked about how relatable their video was for many people.

Since COVID-19, video conferencing has become much more popular, so Tripp and Tyler made another video highlighting their unique issues; some participants were on mute, some had difficulty hearing each another, and some had poor video connections or challenging WIFI issues. Others had people or animals not part of the call appear on the screen, while those calling in from their car had to deal with loud noises and other issues. My favorite part is when the screen freezes at a crucial moment. You could also see people multitasking and sending emails and could hear screaming kids and barking dogs, and so on. The video's ending is the funniest part (which I won't spoil here) and I do recommend watching it until the end because it's something we can all relate to.

Beyond how digital communication has impacted our work/ life balance, because we are constantly in meetings that run over into other meetings, the act of paying attention hour after hour is itself challenging. When we lack effective communication, it impacts our job satisfaction, increases stress, and leads to burnout. But how can we get everything done if we have less digital communication? We need to ask more questions like that one.

As we no longer pass people in the hall where we can ask questions or deliver information because we now work virtually, we continue to schedule meetings that could easily have been replaced by emails or quick calls. Leaders must ask their employees how they like to receive information and what kind of information they would like to receive, whether digitally or over the phone or on a video.

Knowing how to fix communication issues requires first finding out what they are. Asking employees what works for them and what doesn't is a big start. Analyzing turnover data and comparing it to data from exit interviews can help determine the issues with which people struggle. Looking at online sites that rate leadership and how past employees felt about working for your company also generates insights.

Just as organizations should strive to retain customers, they should also strive to retain employees. Not only does employee turnover affect an organization's cohesion and structure, it also costs money. Gallup reports that turnover can range from .5 to 2 times the employee's annual salary, and replacing a C-level position can cost up to 213% of their yearly salary. Indirect costs of low productivity and morale account for two-thirds of that cost. Therefore, uncovering communication barriers is key and requires exercising curiosity by asking questions.

CHAPTER 8

Emotional Intelligence and Empathy

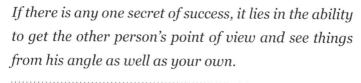

If there is any one secret of success, it lies in the ability to get the other person's point of view and see things from his angle as well as your own.

—Henry Ford

One of my favorite guests on my nationally syndicated radio show was Daniel Goleman, known for his book *Emotional Intelligence: Why It Can Matter More Than IQ*. Goleman was not the first to study emotional intelligence, but he popularized it and made its importance accessible to everyone in the workplace. My interest in emotional intelligence began during my doctoral journey. I wrote my dissertation on the relationship between emotional intelligence and sales performance, and learning all about EI led me to create assessments to quantify the factors that impact curiosity and perception. When I asked Goleman about the value of curiosity at work, he said he believed curiosity was important. I agree. But how exactly does curiosity relate to emotional intelligence?

As defined by Goleman, emotional intelligence is understanding and managing your own emotions *and* recognizing the emotions of others. But how can we do that? We have to ask questions as well as explore and develop empathy. Empathy is the ability to understand and even feel another's feelings. It is the key soft skill that enables us to view another person's emotions through their vantage point. To sense and imagine what someone else feels can be challenging. My co-author (of *The Power of Perception*) Dr. Maja Zelihic and I quickly learned how much our perception impacts our empathy. Our culture, upbringing, sexual orientation, and so many other factors contribute to our emotions, our viewpoints, and how well we recognize emotions in others. However, sometimes the assumptions we make about how others feel can be off base.

I asked Goleman for an example of someone with empathy, and he mentioned Bill Clinton. While some people might find his choice surprising, especially considering some of Clinton's emotionally unintelligent past choices, Goleman explained that people can have high levels of emotional intelligence in some areas and low levels in others. He believed Clinton could make people feel like they were the center of his universe when he spoke to them. People thought he understood their message and their needs. Clinton used eye contact to demonstrate his undivided attention and genuine interest in their problems. He asked many questions and listened, using what he learned to create meaningful dialogue, which helped others feel special.

When employees feel respected and heard, their willingness to work and be productive increases. Many leaders mistakenly treat people how the leader would like to be treated, following the golden rule. However, the 'platinum rule' created by entrepreneur Tony Alessandra has much more impact. His platinum rule holds that we should treat others how *they* wish to be treated. Again, to know how to do that, we must first develop empathy, and to do *that*, we must ask questions by developing our curiosity about those people.

Another guest on my show was Dr. Olin Oedekoven, who has since passed. He was an inspiring man who led a successful education-based organization and whose leadership style was this: he did not assume how others felt about doing their job. He hired people because he saw something in them that he believed would benefit his organization. He encouraged them to work in multiple roles, and only after he had learned how they felt about doing certain tasks and having specific responsibilities did he design their job description.

Employees found working for him enjoyable, challenging, and motivating, and they loved having an increased opportunity to explore personal development. Oedekoven developed empathy for his employees through that discovery journey.

In my failed pharmaceutical sales presentation described above, I never asked the doctor questions or learned anything about him. Consider the difference it would have made had I noticed his pictures of his family or noted where he had studied and asked about those things. What if I asked him what his patient issues were, which may have related to what my product could improve. I could have asked him how he felt about receiving phone calls from suffering patients in the middle of the night. By having honest conversations with people, rather than canned, one-sided presentations, we can learn about their emotions and develop empathy for them.

Some believe that having empathy means one must agree with people or feel everything the same way they do. We certainly don't have to agree with other people's perspectives or perceptions, but we should respect and understand them. That is the true value of empathy.

Low levels of empathy are tied to employee disengagement. Employers who lack empathy lose their best employees. The inability to recognize emotions has hurt marketing campaigns that cost companies dearly.

Consider the Gillette campaign that called out men for their toxic masculinity. Was their intent to be socially aware and have a positive impact? Probably. Was that the outcome? Not exactly; there was quite a backlash as their ad tried to channel the #MeToo movement. They had not considered that such an ad might offend their primary customers, men. The backlash resulted in customers boycotting their products. They defended their ad, stating that discussing the problem could lead to real change. The controversy helped the campaign and garnered attention, which was their intent. Although they had to turn off the dislike button on their YouTube video, they kept the video active.

There are mixed online statements about the aftermath of that controversial campaign. Would having empathy have improved their outcome? Possibly. Would it have been as contentious? Maybe not. But there was a lesson here about the difference between assuming what others want to hear and what they actually want to hear. Whenever we lack empathy and upset our customers, there is always an impact.

Contrast this with how Tylenol responded when their product was tampered with and caused deaths.

Johnson & Johnson, the makers of Tylenol, took an empathetic approach. They considered the fear people were experiencing and created a strategy team to ask questions like "How do we protect the people?" and "How do we save this product?" By removing the product, they showed empathy for the public's safety. By asking questions, they created a triple safety sealed package. How Johnson & Johnson handled the Tylenol scare is now a case study in how to handle a crisis. When organizations demonstrate sympathy based on empathy, it resonates with their customers.

Whether utilizing curiosity to ask questions in a sales presentation to uncover hidden concerns, pain points or other issues, or using curiosity and empathy to respond to a crisis, organizations that demonstrate empathy end up the winner. I am asked if, during a sales presentation, a customer might ask a question that kills the sale, because sometimes a question can reveal that the product is not a good fit for them. Of course, it is always better to find out that a product is not right for a customer prior to the sale. Unhappy customers often give negative reviews, and more damage can be done by not asking questions and failing to see that the customer was not a good fit than by losing a sale.

Asking questions to prepare for an unforeseen crisis is also critical to sales. Had Johnson & Johnson responded differently by not asking the questions they asked, they might have come across as callous and uncaring. But they were able to use what they learned from their quick response to avoid future issues. By recognizing our customers' expectations and emotions, we build long-lasting relationships that encourage them to share their positive stories.

Developing emotional intelligence, including empathy and interpersonal communication skills, has significant benefits. When writing my dissertation on the impact of EI on sales performance, I anticipated that EI would be widely used in future training and development programs. What continues to surprise and dismay me is that since Goleman's 1995 book, I have run into so many organizations whose employees have not even heard of emotional intelligence. According to a 2024 Gitnux market data report, only 42% of companies train employees to cultivate emotional intelligence. Organizations that embrace a culture of curiosity can build emotional intelligence through asking questions and thus improve empathy and understanding.

CHAPTER 9

Motivation

We keep moving forward, opening new doors, and doing new things, because we're curious and curiosity keeps leading us down new paths.

—Walt Disney

I am often asked which comes first, curiosity or motivation. On my show, I have asked that question to many motivational experts, some of whom have written wonderful books on motivation. Without fail, all of them said that curiosity comes first.

I like Dan Pink's book *Drive: The Surprising Truth About What Motivates Us* because it addresses two of the most common ways we motivate ourselves and others: the carrot and the stick. I have found that to have genuine motivation, you need to light the spark of curiosity first. No amount of carrots or beatings with a stick could get me to like some of the jobs I have had simply because I just wasn't interested in them. To be motivated, we need to choose a task that aligns with our interests and capabilities. But how do we develop those? We do that by developing our curiosity and exploring tasks and activities. And to do so we must first address the things that keep us from being curious.

We must be curious and explore what motivates us. Instead, I see many square pegs trying to force themselves into round holes. Although no one is going to love every aspect of their job—someone has to clean the toilets and do the paperwork—surprisingly, some people find motivation in what seems unappealing to others.

My husband *loves* to clean the house. He gets down on his hands and knees and scrubs the floors like it is some kind of challenge. I, on the other hand, am not motivated to do that, and I don't see the joy in scrubbing that he does. However, there are plenty of instances where people have found hard jobs rewarding simply by changing their perception of them.

Consider the Fish! Philosophy modeled after Seattle's Pike Place Fish Market, where employees have fun doing a job that most consider smelly and unappealing. Those who work at the Fish Market have learned to incorporate play, being there, making their day, and choosing their attitude to keep upbeat. By questioning how to make this job better, they learned that tossing the fish to each other made the job more fun while it also entertained the customers.

Research has found that curiosity fosters learning, memory retention, and intrinsic motivation. We know that curiosity lights up the dopamine receptors and makes us feel good, and when we feel good, we find reasons to do the things that we don't do when we feel bad. Curiosity drives us to reduce uncertainty and also provides us with intrinsic motivation, which in turn fosters learning and exploring for their own sake.

Others often ask me how technology has impacted our curiosity and motivation to learn. That is a valid concern given that search engines, AI, and other devices often answer our questions as quickly as we can ask them. However, getting answers quickly and easily can limit our critical thinking skills. If we too often take one source as gospel, that can reinforce our confirmation bias. And when we think we know all the answers, our motivation to undertake more research can disappear.

That is where I like to challenge those who feel that getting quick answers from technology is the best way.

There is a reason professors like me prohibit their students from citing Wikipedia and similar sources. First, those sites are sometimes inaccurate. That is why digging deeper to find and cite primary sources is so critical. Being motivated to dig deeper requires curiosity about whether that answer is correct. This is where I see many people struggle. They find it easier to convince themselves that the information on these sites is correct than to do actual, primary research. We can improve our motivation to explore if we uncover what we tell ourselves about that data. Later in this book I will discuss part of what improves our curiosity as well as the four factors that inhibit it. For now, the four factors of FATE (fear, assumptions, technology, and environment) can hold us back from exploring what we think we know, what we think is too much trouble to do, and what we tell ourselves. When I cover these factors later and in more detail, I will share how to overcome them. For now, let's consider what we tell ourselves and see how that impacts our curiosity and, ultimately, our motivation.

When we are motivated, we are more engaged at work. In the U.S., we lose $550 billion a year in lost productivity. Curiosity is critical because it improves motivation. We need to recognize that engagement is about an emotional connection and commitment to a job, both of which improve when we are free to explore and ask questions at work. That emotional connection and commitment gives us the energy to act, which is exactly what motivation is. And it is curiosity that improves and sparks both.

For example, some workers are motivated by bonuses to take action. But once they receive that bonus, they can lose that incentive to be motivated. Sparking curiosity can be thought of as a bonus that never goes away because it leads us to be motivated, which in turn also leads us to be engaged.

CHAPTER 10

Productivity

Curiosity leads to new ideas, new jobs, new industries.

—Anne Sweeney

By improving curiosity, we can become more engaged and innovative, which naturally increases our productivity. For instance, if we want to bake a cake, we must do more than just mix the ingredients and put them in a pan; we must also turn on the oven to turn the mix into a cake. In the same way, to help employees be more productive (our organization's version of the cake) we must spark their curiosity to ensure the raw ingredients yield our desired outcome. And so, when we ignite the spark of curiosity, we ignite motivation. Because when employees feel passion for what they do, their productivity improves, which is the financial outcome leaders seek.

I have found that although leaders see the value of curiosity, they also worry that it could cause distractions. Leaders also *think* they encourage curiosity in their employees, but often those same employees would not agree. If leaders want to improve their bottom line—which is always their eventual goal— they must accept and initiate culture change.

In her *Harvard Business Review* article, Elizabeth Grace Saunders shared that leaders need to identify specific steps and goals to improve productivity and then use their curiosity to reach those goals. When we develop our curiosity we become better problem-solvers. Curiosity can also improve work relationships and reduce stress, both of which can improve productivity, leading to employees who feel empowered and are more committed to their work. And when that happens, their job satisfaction improves and they become more productive.

Building curiosity increases our perception of psychological safety. And when employees feel psychologically safe, innovation improves, along with their creativity, problem-solving, and loyalty, among other factors.

Lighting that spark of curiosity opens up a world of possibilities. When organizations experience low productivity, the quality of their goods and services worsens, their labor costs increase, they become less competitive, and because of increased worker stress and burnout their healthcare costs increase.

If everyone agrees intuitively that developing curiosity can improve a host of business concerns, then why do so many organizations fail to train their employees in this area? One of the biggest problems is that curiosity is such a subjective and squishy word. It can be hard to define because it involves cognition and emotional and behavioral aspects.

I found the same to be true when studying emotional intelligence. I wanted to make sure the assessment I chose incorporated a definition of emotional intelligence that I agreed with, so I tested multiple assessments before choosing the one I used for my research.

It can also be challenging to measure curiosity's short-term impact on productivity. I worked with a doctoral student who researched curiosity's effect on productivity within an organization. First, they measured curiosity levels via an assessment like Kashdan's (see Appendix), then they provided curiosity training, and then they again measured curiosity levels to see if they had improved. I would like to see more organizations do research to demonstrate the link between improving curiosity and the benefits of improved innovation, engagement, and other factors that improve productivity.

Curiosity's impact on productivity can also vary by industry, culture, and type of organizational structure (i.e., hierarchical or flat). Because different leaders define and embrace curiosity differently, curiosity's effect on productivity can be challenging to interpret. The majority of leaders I've worked with intuitively saw a connection between curiosity and productivity. If you are in the minority who need more data to prove this connection, read the results I share in the following chapters that will tell you all about specific organizations.

* * *

Metrics:

The working world uses a variety of metrics to gauge economic and business performance. Some metrics include key performance indicators (KPIs), which measure factors over time that affect product sales or subscriber growth. Another metric is objectives and key results (OKRs), which outline measurable steps to achieve goals. OKRs, which have been popularized by Google and Intel, provide a strategic framework. An example of an OKR might be ensuring everyone is working toward common goals by limiting objectives, ensuring transparency, setting ambitious goals (that require accountability), adjusting, and providing feedback.

KPIs

To create an effective KPI, leaders need to use curiosity to ensure that business objectives align with the organization's strategic priorities. A curiosity-based culture can help produce innovative and creative KPIs. For example, curiosity can improve product development, time-to-market, and revenue from new products when leaders and workers explore innovative solutions and solve problems in new ways. Curiosity-based problem-solving resolves issues more effectively, more easily identifies process improvements and efficiencies, and stimulates workers and leaders to better streamline their workflows.

A curiosity mindset can eventually improve customer satisfaction because it generates feedback that helps businesses improve and adapt. A constant desire to learn more about people also improves employee training, skill development, and performance, as it creates a learning organization that improves KPIs related to employee development.

Curiosity and the idea-sharing it generates helps businesses in an ever-changing environment to change and adapt to market trends while they improve their collaboration and team performance. This in turn leads to better quality products and services, which are vital to keeping businesses competitive.

When creating KPIs, curiosity-inspired leaders will encourage questioning, provide learning opportunities, celebrate and reward contributions, create a culture that values exploration, and lead by example. They do this last step by asking questions, providing feedback, and showing a commitment to learning.

Let's consider the following examples of organizations that used curiosity when creating their KPIs.

Google's KPI of employee satisfaction and innovation was improved by curiosity because they encouraged employees to spend 20% of their time on personal projects, which led to innovations such as Gmail and Google Maps, among others.

Examples abound showing how curiosity improved some of the biggest names in business. Curiosity works, whether it drives Apple's KPI of product sales by improving their commitment to design and innovation, or it helps Amazon create a seamless buying process to enhance its KPI of operational efficiency and customer experience.

OKRs

OKRs (and KPIs) can help organizations measure if curiosity is helping them reach their productivity goals. Because when they can measure that improvement, it's easier for them to foster a culture of curiosity. Businesses can then use a curiosity-based approach to define ambitious, qualitative, and inspirational objectives to create practical objectives and key results (OKRs). In this way, curiosity can then help organizations create breakthroughs, be more innovative, pioneer solutions, and so on.

For instance, an OKR for Google might be to pioneer a next-generation technology by launching two experimental projects: one to encourage employees to dedicate 20% of their time to self-directed projects, and another to host internal innovation fairs to reward curiosity-driven projects.

A curiosity-inspired OKR for any other organization might include enhancing employee learning and development. They could achieve this by increasing training hours by 20%, achieving a 90% class completion rate, and surveying employees quarterly and achieving a satisfaction score of 85%.

Frameworks, Methodologies, and Concepts:
SMART

SMART goals are Specific, Measurable, Achievable, Relevant, and Time-bound. A SMART goal for Google might be to improve its search engine's user engagement. A curiosity-driven approach might be to use behavior data to create innovative features. Teams would use curiosity to define the engagement aspects clearly in order to make them specific. To make the improvement measurable, Google's teams would need to choose how much longer the average session duration would need to be, whether 15% or some other figure. To make the improvement achievable, Google would have the ability to implement the changes. To make the improvement relevant, the goal would have to align with Google's business objectives, and to make it time-bound, the improvement would need to have a specific deadline or time limit set for it, such as 'the next six months'.

SWOT

Curiosity is also necessary to create a SWOT analysis. SWOT stands for Strengths, Weaknesses, Opportunities, and Threats, all of which can impact an organization. Disney might use curiosity in their SWOT to create a new theme park, and to do so they would have to ask questions and seek information. This might include finding out how their brand recognition and loyalty could be a strength. Disney could also ask how much strain the initial investment in such a park might create and if one of their weaknesses is adapting to new cultures. They could also inquire about untapped markets and what threats exist from competition, regulation, or economic volatility.

Curiosity helps drive the success of metrics. Whether this happens by asking questions for SMART goals or a SWOT analysis, by determining the return on an investment (ROI), or by querying a variety of other acronyms and abbreviations that organizations use, curiosity is at the heart of each successful outcome. In short, curiosity works.

PART III

WHAT ORGANIZATIONS ARE DOING

Curiosity has emerged as a common thread through the success stories of some of the largest companies worldwide. While I will explore the specific actions and strategies employed by these organizations in detail in the upcoming pas, the overarching theme is curiosity's pivotal role in shaping their trajectories.

Verizon, Novartis, Google, Disney, Great Ormond Street Hospital, Ben & Jerry's, Vanmoof, GE, and LEGO are not merely conglomerates; they exemplify how fostering a culture of curiosity can propel organizations to unparalleled heights. Curiosity is not just a desirable trait within these corporate giants; it is the driving force permeating their organizational DNA.

Organizations like Verizon understand that curiosity is not a passive attribute but an active catalyst for innovation and growth. It fuels a dynamic environment that encourages employees to explore new ideas, question the status quo, and contribute meaningfully to the company's evolution. This mindset is not exclusive to tech behemoths like Google; instead, it resonates across industries, from healthcare giants like Novartis to entertainment pioneers like Disney.

Regarding social impact, institutions like Great Ormond Street Hospital recognize that curiosity is not confined to the boardroom; it extends to every facet of their mission to heal and nurture. Similarly, companies like Ben & Jerry's leverage curiosity to help them listen to their customers in order to create successful products.

Innovative products and sustainable practices find common ground among companies like Vanmoof, GE, and LEGO. These organizations understand that curiosity is about asking questions and actively seeking solutions that redefine industries and contribute to a sustainable future.

Curiosity underpins the success of these global entities. When businesses recognize that curiosity is not a luxury but a strategic imperative, it can help shape their organizational culture, fuel innovation, and drive them toward continued excellence. These companies' stories can serve as compelling evidence that curiosity isn't just a value-add; it's an indispensable force that propels organizations toward a future defined by exploration, innovation, and enduring success.

CHAPTER 11

Verizon

People had a chance to talk to us. All our leaders solicited information. What binds people together is a mission or a purpose that's bigger than themselves.

—Ivan Seidenberg

One of my favorite things is to share what organizations have done to demonstrate a culture of curiosity. I helped Verizon create videos about how they valued curiosity, which they shared with their employees and potential new hires. These videos showcased how curiosity impacted their employees' success. I loved that Verizon shared these videos with their employees during their onboarding process and then played them throughout their internal network.

The videos included a few minutes of me speaking about the value of curiosity during which I shared my background and expertise on what curiosity could help them achieve. This was followed by testimonials from select employees who shared how curiosity helped them succeed in their job. In the videos, they referred to their culture as "My Edge" and spoke about how curiosity ties into creativity and innovation.

When people are asked to make cultural changes, they must know why. What's in it for them? In these Verizon videos I also explained the four factors of FATE that inhibit curiosity, which we will explore in more depth later on. Sharing these factors has been critical to the successful launch of building a culture of curiosity.

I particularly liked that Verizon's videos included examples of employees who had used curiosity to succeed. In one video, a salesperson talked about how she overcame challenges within her environment. She was born in Mexico and raised in a traditional family that did not embrace education for women. As you might recall, the E in FATE (from taking the Curiosity Code Index assessment) stands for environment.

Our environment includes all the people with whom we have interacted. She shared how she leaned into her curiosity—and this led to her success. She paid for her own education, which was challenging. She initially hesitated to take on additional leadership responsibilities due to her environmental impact, which led to the A in FATE, which stands for assumptions (that voice in our head that tells us we can't or shouldn't do something). This in turn led to her F in FATE, which stands for fear. Verizon's culture allowed her to share her insights, which gave her the confidence to assume a leadership role, and now she encourages curiosity in her team.

Verizon shares with their workers how they embrace a culture of curiosity and encourages them to ask "What if?"

"Why?" and "How might we?" They also encourage their employees to share Verizon's designated hashtag on social media about how curiosity could drive their employees' work forward. They continue to share examples of successful employees, how their culture developed women in STEM, and how their innovative free training program helps millions of students thrive. Whether they have created Voice over LTE programs to create higher-quality voice calls, video-chat capabilities, or many other innovative products, Verizon promotes forging ahead without fear. Their people learn through their mistakes. Although they initially missed being Apple iPhone's exclusive wireless provider, Verizon has used curiosity to develop other business avenues. Sometimes, our losses can lead to the next big opportunity. Harvard Professor Rosabeth Moss Kanter calls it Kanter's Law: "In the middle, everything looks like a failure." "But," she explained, "that is where the hard work happens. It is part of the process of any change."

CHAPTER 12

Novartis

We believe curiosity drives discovery. We know curiosity solves problems. We are convinced that curiosity powers innovation. We all need curiosity to learn.

—Novartis website

I have alluded previously that Novartis, a large pharmaceutical organization, has worked to create a culture of curiosity. Novartis fortunately included me in many of their exploration and learning opportunities to help their employees embrace curiosity. One of my favorite things Novartis does is pay for their employees to receive 100 hours of educational opportunities each year.

Additionally, Novartis has initiated Curiosity Month, during which they bring in hundreds of speakers and allow employees to choose the training sessions they find most valuable and exciting. I enjoyed participating in these events and found that their employees asked insightful questions because they didn't fear repercussions for doing so. Incredibly, Novartis also provides mini TEDx-like talks, but instead of hiring speakers to deliver those talks, they have their own employees share their insights. If you have ever taught, you know that there is no better way to learn something than to teach it to others. When employees share what they have learned, their confidence and knowledge grows, especially when they teach fellow employees who are unfamiliar with their topic.

While I was helping Novartis, I was fortunate to forge a relationship with their former CMO Simon Brown, who wrote the book *The Curious Advantage* with co-authors Paul Ashcroft and Garrick Jones.

The Curious Advantage explores the behavior surrounding curiosity as well as curiosity's central role in the digital age. The book explores every facet of curiosity, including historical, contemporary, neuro-scientific, anthropological, behavioral, and business aspects. The three authors also host a curiosity-based podcast named after the book.

Simon Brown has since moved on from Novartis, but he left an indelible mark. Their culture embraces curiosity to the extent that their website states the following:

"We believe curiosity drives discovery. We know curiosity solves problems. We are convinced that curiosity powers innovation. We all need curiosity to learn. Novartis aspires to offer the best learning and development opportunities to instill this curiosity."

Novartis reinforces their curiosity culture by explaining that effective learning is intentional and requires removing barriers and encouraging skill development. Novartis pays for thousands of courses from Coursera and LinkedIn learning, which allows their employees to develop new skills and ways of working.

Novartis has also researched how developing curiosity ties into improved engagement. They measured curiosity levels prior to some of their culturally based curiosity training and then measured them again afterwards, correlating that with engagement. They found that their training moved the needle! Considering the staggering cost of low engagement, I am impressed that an organization that values curiosity so highly conducts research to support it. I hope that more organizations will do the same—or more—and also publish their findings.

Novartis's valuing of curiosity also spills over into their code of ethics, because being open-minded is first on their list of ethical principles. They encourage employees to ask questions like

- Am I actively listening to ideas or concerns?
- Am I valuing others' perspectives?
- Am I acting with clear intent?
- Am I avoiding harm?
- Am I speaking up?
- Am I standing up for what I believe?
- Am I putting patients first?
- Am I making a positive difference?
- Am I taking responsibility for my decisions?
- Am I treating others as I would like to be treated?
- Am I putting the team before myself?

All of these are fundamental questions. But if I could tweak one of them, it would be to change, "Am I treating others as *I* would like to be treated?" to "Am I treating others as *they* would like to be treated?" which Tony Alessandra has coined as the 'platinum rule', making it one of the most critical questions to ask.

CHAPTER 13

Google

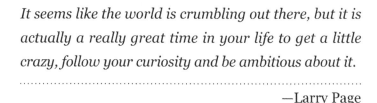

It seems like the world is crumbling out there, but it is actually a really great time in your life to get a little crazy, follow your curiosity and be ambitious about it.

—Larry Page

Google's "20% time" rule made it one of the most cited examples of organizations that encourage curiosity. In their IPO letter, founders Sergey Brin and Larry Page wrote,

"We encourage our employees, in addition to their regular projects, to spend 20% of their time working on what they think will most benefit Google."

Some now debate whether Google still encourages this rule and just how formal it is. However, Brin and Page have credited many of their discoveries to this rule, claiming,

"This empowers [our employees] to be more creative and innovative. Many of our significant advances [like AdSense and Google News] have happened in this manner."

Whether they continue to use it or not, Google's rule is an excellent example of an organization striving to be more curious, creative, and innovative. Google says that AdSense came about thanks to this rule. In 2022, Google's $224.47 billion revenue came primarily through advertising, of which $32.8 billion came through AdSense alone. Google also has credited 20% time for making Gmail more revenue-positive. Gmail generates income from personalized ads that retarget users based on their online activity. Google's rule led Apple, LinkedIn, and many other organizations to implement similar rules. For instance, Apple's Blue Sky program allows employees time to work on pet projects.

Google continues to experiment with ways to develop curiosity, whether through the 20% time rule, Google Labs, or a host of other initiatives. Are they all successful? That depends on how you define success. Did projects get created that made them money? Yes! Did they learn from the demise of some of their projects? Yes! Sometimes, people can get spread too thin, and not all ideas become home runs—but has Google maintained a culture of curiosity? Most definitely!

For over a quarter of a century, Google has grown through innovations like Google Maps; acquiring companies like YouTube, Fitbit, and Android; launching the AI-powered chatbot Bard; and by expanding their brand to become Alphabet. Google is so ubiquitous that their very name has become a verb. While some Google projects, like Google Glasses, have not succeeded, the company continues to innovate. Google's AI platform Bard produces multiple answers to one query and simulates human conversations, thus taking curiosity to a new level. Google's technological advances come to fruition so quickly that by the time this book is published they will have surpassed whatever advances I mention here. One thing is certain; Google continues to innovate and use curiosity to stay relevant and dominate the technology space.

CHAPTER 14

Disney

Having a deep and abiding curiosity enables the discovery of new people, places, and ideas (i.e., business ventures). Curiosity also helps leaders gain awareness and an understanding of the marketplace and its changing dynamics. The path to innovation begins with curiosity.

—Bob Iger

Disney and its products have gone through many incarnations since the company's inception in 1923. One of the things Disney does best is to embrace curiosity, which leads to creativity. When writing about curiosity, you might expect a story about how Disney discovered Mickey Mouse or developed top-grossing movies. Instead, I would like to share an issue more relatable to many organizations.

Consider how Disney overcame the problem of low engagement in their laundry division. Not everything you see at Disneyland is glamorous. Just ask the people who work in the laundry. Cleaning and ironing linens is even more dull and boring than it sounds, and because of how hard the work was, Disney found that they were losing many people. The turnover was so high that Disney sent out a questionnaire to determine what they could do to improve those jobs for their workers. They asked them, "What can we do to make your job better?" They also asked, "What changes would you recommend to serve our guests better?" They expected to receive comments that were above and beyond what they had the desire and/or finances to accommodate; however, Disney soon learned that employees needed but a few small accommodations to become more engaged.

For example, Disney's machines, which automatically folded sheets and towels, had bands that moved the sheets and towels forward. But the bands often broke, which halted the whole process. To the question about how to make their job better, Disney received practical answers like, "Put an air vent over my workspace" and "Make my folding table adjustable for my height." To the question about how to serve guests better, one of the cast members (what Disney calls their theme park employees) suggested using a knot, one that he had learned when serving in the Navy, to secure the ends of a broken band.

Leaders listened and made changes. Disney shared how they incorporated their employees' feedback and how significant their contributions were to the company. And it worked! Disney lowered its annual employee turnover from 85% to less than 10% just by making a few simple changes. The resulting annual cost savings totaled over $100,000!

Another example of curiosity-inspired success at Disney came from a company they acquired. I didn't read many comic books as a kid, but every once in a while I liked to read *Spi-*

der-Man. I also remember liking the movie *Spider-Man* with Toby Maguire when it came out in 2002. Since then, creator Marvel has been on fire! Founded in 1938 by Martin Goodman, Marvel was initially known as Timely Publications. Although at first successful, it waned after World War II. But then in the 1960s, Stan Lee became the editor and introduced such iconic characters as the Fantastic Four, which launched Marvel's storytelling of complex characters. Stan's curiosity to explore interconnected universes was a success.

Over-estimating the demand for their comic books, they had mistakenly printed too many and had run into trouble. They bounced back from their problems when their strategic leadership used curiosity to explore new opportunities by following trends based on consumer desires. They expanded into film and television in 1993 with Marvel Studios and brought their characters to life, capturing a broader audience. They encouraged their filmmakers and writers to explore different genres and storytelling styles, and they capitalized on their interconnected storylines, which appealed to fans.

In 2009, The Walt Disney Company acquired Marvel Entertainment for $4 billion, providing them with additional resources and opportunities for expansion. By 2021, Marvel was valued at $53 billion.

Disney further utilized curiosity to grow Marvel by exploring intellectual property beyond comic books, expanding the boundaries of storytelling, allowing creative teams to experiment, engaging with passionate fans, embracing technological advancements in filmmaking (including special effects), and exploring diverse content platforms like television.

CHAPTER 15

Great Ormond Street Hospital

"What could go wrong?" and "What are we going to do if it does go wrong?" and "How important is it if it goes wrong?"

—Formula One Pit Crew
at Great Ormond Street Hospital

Hospitals seldom come to mind when one thinks about curiosity-based organizations. However, they experience the same need for innovation and improvement as other organizations. A 2005 study found that nearly 70% of preventable hospital mishaps occurred because of communication problems, and other studies have shown that at least half of such breakdowns occur while moving patients from one location to another.

London's Great Ormond Street Hospital, which treats heart patients, was experiencing an inordinate number of casualties when they were transferring patients from one unit to another. Physicians watching a Formula One race one day were impressed by how quickly and efficiently the pit crews serviced everything, error-free, in seven seconds or less. So, they invited a Formula

One racing team to come in and view the hospital's transfer procedures and then make observations based on their processes. Twenty-one surgeons across Britain allowed the Ferrari crew to observe their operations. The team explained how their pit crew used a system for recording errors that might typically go unnoticed. The pit stops were successful because of their attention to these tiny mistakes.

Each member of the Ferrari crew had a specific job to do, unlike the hospital team, where no jobs were permanently assigned. Instead, during transfers, nurses and doctors carried on separate conversations while the other members of the team were less than connected to what was happening. The anesthesiologist usually took charge of the handover, but at times it was the surgeon and sometimes no one was in charge. The hospital teams worried only about problems after encountering them. However, once the hospital implemented the process that the racing team recommended, their errors decreased dramatically; the average number of technical mistakes per handover fell by 42%, and "information handover omissions" fell by 49%. Each transfer also took slightly less time to execute, even though the doctors weren't trying to speed up their process—unlike the Ferrari team.

Because Great Ormond's team was curious and thus open to new perspectives, they thought outside the box and consulted with the Ferrari team, which happened because the hospital shed their status-quo behaviors. Thus, curiosity can break silos, as it drives people outside their comfort zone.

So, how can you develop this skill? You might start by routinely reaching out to new people and disciplines—anyone outside your usual circles—which can open your mind and enable you to be more creative and find solutions you might have never considered.

CHAPTER 16

Ben & Jerry's

I'd rather fail at something new than succeed at something old.

....

—Ben Cohen and Jerry Greenfield

One company that often comes to mind when discussing innovation is Ben and Jerry's because they are willing to shed what is no longer successful. They literally bury their old flavors by holding a business funeral for them, going as far as to assign the defunct flavor a grave plot and an actual tombstone (their website has pictures of this gravesite). For example, you might see a flavor with a date span of 1993 to 2001, when that flavor was successful, but now it lies buried because it is no longer popular. Ben Cohen and Jerry Greenfield do not lament the loss of an idea. They recognize it was a great idea in its day, but now it's time to move on to bigger and better things. They understand that products have lives with a beginning and end. Hanging onto products past their expiration date, they realized, can be ineffective—and costly.

After a decade of solid sales, for example, Ben & Jerry's reluctantly retired their White Russian flavor in 1996, but not because it was unpopular. The cost of the Kahlua-like flavoring used in its production had become prohibitive. They have repurposed funds that were once spent on old flavors and use them to invest in new ideas. This strategy has been very successful, and today they still move some of their once best-selling flavors onto the great waffle cone in the sky, otherwise known as their Flavor Graveyard.

They use quizzes on their website to gather customer information to help focus their marketing efforts. They pique customers' curiosity with questions like "What pint holds the secret to your high school persona?" and then follow with questions about their favorite things in high school, with the answers resulting in a suggested ice cream flavor.

While many organizations failed to thrive during the pandemic, Ben & Jerry's created 40 new products, which made 2020 their most innovative year ever. Employees are encouraged to suggest flavor ideas based on their childhood memories, the holidays, or other experiences that spark their curiosity and creativity. If you've ever had chocolate chip cookie dough ice cream, you should know that Ben & Jerry's created that flavor in their scoop shop in Vermont in 1984. This ingenious flavor was invented thanks to a suggestion left on their anonymous flavor suggestion board. Today, they churn up 194,164,241 pints of ice cream per year, and chocolate chip cookie dough is one of their most popular flavors, averaging over 1.5 million pints each year. Consider the impact of just asking for input on a suggestion board!

CHAPTER 17

VanMoof

Take risks, stay curious and go for it.

—Martien Mellema VanMoof website

Another example of thinking outside the box comes from VanMoof, a hybrid electric bike company. The company found that their bikes were getting damaged at a very high rate during shipping. They brainstormed how to fix this, but every idea they came up with, like using thicker packaging, cost more money. Rather than just give up, they thought about what goods don't break during shipping. They noticed that flat screens are shipped in packages similar to their own every day all over the world without much damage. They used their curiosity to ask how this was possible. They then noticed that the flat-screen TVs always had a picture of the TV on the box, so they decided to print an image of a flat-screen TV on their bikes' boxes. It cost them a little extra—but damage rates decreased by 70%.

VanMoof has struggled as well, and even after raising over $225 million in venture capital they eventually went bankrupt. However, they have continued to ask questions to find ways to continue their operations and expand into more areas of e-mobility. For instance, they are planning to launch VanMoof 2.0, replacing retail parts with in-house repair shops and a new e-scooter. Their lessons from past failures have sent them on new paths, and they recognize that hanging onto status-quo ways caused Kodak and Blockbuster to fail. Going forward, they intend to use firmware to update product bugs and move away from servicing and adhere instead to their core manufacturing mission.

Of course, they must ask why they failed. Was it because they did not use regular bike parts and created their own, which broke, leading to maintenance shops that could not keep up with the issues? Was it because they ran out of money as they waited to become the next unicorn? Was it because of the high upfront costs they paid for research and development? Was it due to supply chain and quality control issues? Was it because their product quality and reliability did not match their marketing hype? Or was it all of the above? They need to answer these and other questions now if they wish to achieve their desired comeback.

CHAPTER 18

GE

An organization's ability to learn, and translate that learning into action rapidly, is the ultimate competitive advantage.

—Jack Welch

GE encourages curiosity in the workplace by providing employees with "GE Garages," where employees can collaborate with other companies and researchers to explore new technologies and business models. For example, by encouraging this behavior, GE produced the first fully 3D-printed working miniature jet engine. They also created 3D parts for appliances that reduced development time by 80%. In addition, GE Healthcare created the "GE Healthcare Technology Center," where employees can spend time focusing on their interests and then align those interests with the organization's overall goals.

GE has long been viewed as an innovative organization. They transformed into a digital leader by using software and sensors to connect their machines and improve responsiveness. They have utilized edge computing—a distributed computing model that is an alternative to cloud computing—because it is faster and brings computation and data storage closer to the sources of. GE did this to enhance the capabilities and performance of billions of machines and systems. Why did they use edge computing when the cloud might have the answers? They likely asked: What can't be done in the cloud that can be done better through the edge?

Jack Welch, known for being insatiably curious, was sometimes criticized for exploring new horizons and earned the moniker "Neutron Jack." But as revenues increased, his style gained attention. He spent much time finding the right people and didn't hesitate to let underperformers go. Although he was criticized for choosing his successor and for how he treated people, he was always candid—some say to the point of cruelty. But he defended his choices. Which was crueler: keeping someone who was underperforming or letting them go?

Love him or hate him, he embraced one crucial mindset: being insatiably curious. In an *HBR* article, Claudio Fernández-Aráoz recounted his experience of having Jack at his home for a dinner party in Argentina. Jack spent the evening asking Claudio's friends, "How do you have this crazy inflation?" "How can you forecast, plan, and even decide to carry on an investment?"

While Jack Welch receives many accolades for what he did for GE, he was not the only one to embrace curiosity. Their CMO, Beth Comstock, credits curiosity for propelling her forward. She explained that to succeed in business, you must be competitive and said two things made her comfortable with embracing competition: being confident and curious. She asks questions like, "What's going on?" "How do I uncover what's next?" "What is a need?" and "How do I find out what someone is looking for?"

She said that curiosity gave her the courage to explore and understand. Her next step was to try new things, beginning with something small and build from there. Being curious sometimes means that you have to put yourself in uncomfortable situations. For introverts, this may mean having to attend networking events and meeting new people. Comstock said that she overcame her fear by using curiosity—which propelled her forward.

GE offers multiple examples of employees who have used curiosity to succeed. One of them is engineer Colin Parris, who blends art and science to transform curiosity into innovation. His Digital Twin Initiative combined physics and artificial intelligence to emulate the human brain. Parris calls it a "living, learning model." Like a jet engine with a twin, it can warn when something should be optimized or replaced and can provide more comprehensive calculations than a human brain. To create his innovative discoveries, Parris tapped into his childhood experiences in Trinidad, his travels, and everything he had read about early examples of technology and societies. Drawing on diverse experiences and a relentless curiosity can lead to revolutionary innovations that push the boundaries of technology and industry.

Time will tell what outcome the splitting of GE into two companies will reveal. However, GE's consistent emphasis on fostering curiosity within its ranks illustrates a foundational truth: curiosity is not just a personal trait but a powerful corporate asset.

CHAPTER 19

LEGO

With a bucket of Legos, you can tell any story. You can build an airplane or a dragon or a pirate ship–it's whatever you can imagine.

—Christopher Miller

I had many toys as a child, but I never owned Legos. However, my neighbors had them and I had fun playing with them at their house. Back then Legos were simple, just a bunch of bricks to click together, but we had fun and used our imagination. Then in the 1980s, Lego, a Danish company, expanded rapidly, sometimes teetering on the edge of failure. Brian Sørensen, LEGO Group Director, used an unconventional approach to develop Lego's management philosophy. He believed there were paradoxes in leadership, including establishing close relationships with employees without getting too close. He valued expressing opinions in diplomatic ways.

Not all has been rosy for Lego. In the early 2000s, they experienced another downturn that threatened their survival, this one caused by too broad an expansion of its product line, a lack of new products, stiffer competition from electronics and video games, an overestimated inventory, and leadership changes. By 2003, Lego was reporting significant losses.

However, they overcame these issues by refocusing on their core products, investing in innovation, reducing costs, improving quality control, and forming strategic partnerships. Moreover, they improved their culture.

Several factors have contributed to creating Lego's culture of curiosity:

- Incorporating play and creativity
- Having open and collaborative workspaces
- Promoting diverse and inclusive teams
- Having innovative labs and workshops
- Encouraging risk-taking and employee development programs
- Taking a customer-centric approach
- Making time for personal projects
- Recognizing employee contributors and supportive leaders who participate in initiatives that promote curiosity

In addition to their traditional brick sets, Lego created products that tied into pop culture and mimicked architecture, robotics, and art. Legoland, their chain of Lego-themed amusement parks, has been successful as well. They opened the first Legoland in Denmark in 1968 and have since built ten more parks worldwide. Thanks to developing their curiosity, as of 2023 Lego is the most valuable toy brand in the world, worth over $7.4 billion.

PART IV

PRODUCTS AND PROCEDURES

Curiosity has emerged as the driving force behind transformative creations that have impacted society. Curiosity is a common denominator in the development of products that have shaped industries and redefined our lives.

One remarkable example of this is the smartphone. Curiosity drove the transformation of primitive mobile phones into today's complex devices. This occurred as we were exploring how communication and technology could seamlessly integrate. The result was a ubiquitous product that has revolutionized how we connect, work, and navigate the world.

Another revolutionary product born out of curiosity is the electric car. Here again, curiosity drove our search for sustainable transportation solutions that would lessen our environmental impact, which led us to develop the electric vehicles now at the forefront of the automotive industry. This innovation reflects the transformative power of curiosity in addressing global challenges.

Wearable technology also owes its existence to curiosity, this time applied to product innovation. Curiosity again drove us to explore how best to integrate technology into our daily lives, which gave rise to fitness trackers, smartwatches, and other products that monitor our health and enhance our connectivity as they redefine personal computing.

In healthcare, CRISPR technology—CRISPR stands for Clustered Regularly Interspaced Short Palindromic Repeats—refers to a family of DNA sequences found in the genomes of organisms such as bacteria, which can be used to perform genome editing (i.e., to ensure a baby is born with a specific eye color). CRISPR's development exemplifies curiosity's profound impact on biotechnological advancements. Curiosity about manipulating DNA drove scientists to explore gene-editing capabilities, which has effected, and will continue to effect, new medical breakthroughs in treating genetic disorders, thus advancing personalized healthcare.

Retail e-commerce platforms have also emerged from curiosity-driven innovation. Curiosity regarding how technology could revolutionize shopping led us to develop platforms that have transformed the retail landscape, offering convenience and accessibility to consumers worldwide.

Not all curiosity-inspired innovations reinvent entire industries, however. Organizations have created some of the most ingenious and practical products utilizing biomimicry. Products like Velcro were created when someone, driven by curiosity, mimicked the natural world. Products like Post-It Notes, Bubble Wrap, and many others were created accidentally out of curiosity. These product innovations testify to curiosity's transformative power in the creative process. All of these stories inspire us to recognize curiosity's pivotal role in pushing the boundaries of creativity and bringing forth inventions that shape our daily lives.

CHAPTER 20

Biomimicry

An understanding of the natural world is a source of
not only great curiosity, but great fulfilment.

—Sir David Attenborough

Biomimicry occurs when people mimic nature, its designs and systems, in order to design, innovate, and solve human problems. Some of our most valuable lessons have come from studying the animals, patterns, and the designs we take for granted in the plant and animal world. Whether we go back to Leonardo da Vinci, who studied bird flight to enable human flight, or look to recent maple seed-inspired biome renewables (that provide renewable energy), endless examples exist of people using their curiosity to create inventions by mimicking what they see in nature.

Biomimicry examples can be essential, profitable, and fun all at the same time. Some products were developed when someone studied the fractal patterns or spirals in whirlpools, tornados, or even seashells. Scientists at Pax Water used this same spiral pattern to develop tank-mixing technology, which reduced energy requirements by 30%.

Some of the best inventions have come from things we consider gross, annoying, or even scary. Have you ever been curious about slime mold? Well, you might be if you knew it could help planners map out complex, but efficient, traffic patterns. In this instance, Japanese engineers placed oat flakes on the ground in various locations to track the feeding of slime mold to determine complex, but efficient, networks of mapping that would have taken years to plan but that took less than six days.

If mosquitoes annoy you, as they do most people, consider what we've learned from them. The next time you give blood at the doctor's office, your experience is less painful because the needle they use on you mimics the three-pronged needle on a mosquito, which evolved to do its job with a minimum of pain.

Not a fan of sharks? Consider how imitating their skin created swimsuits so efficient that the U.S. Olympic swim team banned them after swimmers wearing them won 98% of all gold medals.

If you've ever heard the thud of a bird flying into your glass window, you might be interested in what we've learned from spiders; they also dislike having birds land in their webs, so they incorporate UV-reflective silk to make them more visible. ORNILUX Bird Protection Glass was created using a UV-reflective coating that mimics a spider's silk so that birds can see the glass and avoid flying into it.

Don't love lizards? You might appreciate what we learned from the chameleon, which can change colors to match its environment. Their tongue is two times faster than the fastest car and can grasp prey of different sizes and shapes. Festo created a material that grips soft and flexible silicon patterned after a chameleon's tongue. This invention is used by the military and relief actions when the sizes and shapes of items to be retrieved are unknown.

A Swiss engineer designed Velcro when he noticed that his dog's fur kept accumulating burrs. The Japanese modeled the bullet train after a bird's beak. Wind turbine blade designs were inspired by humpback whale flippers. The Namibian fog-basking beetle inspired water collection systems and geckos inspired adhesives. The list is endless!

So, how can we use our curiosity to study nature, and what can that do for us? We can use our curiosity about how natural ecosystems function, adapt, and sustain themselves and encourage others to design products and systems that are sustainable. We can study communities of bees and ants to learn effective communication, cooperation, and division of labor, which can lead to more diversity in our teams. We can recognize a forest's ability to withstand disturbances to create better risk management practices. By watching swarming birds, we can create robotics that can work together autonomously. And through educating our employees, stakeholders, and communities about the connections made in nature, we can drive curiosity-based learning that fosters an innovative workforce.

CHAPTER 21

Velcro

Aside from Velcro, time is the most mysterious substance in the universe ... Life was meant to be lived, and curiosity must be kept alive.

—Dave Barry

In 1941, Georges de Mestral, a Swiss engineer, was hunting with his dog in the hills of Switzerland and became annoyed when he returned home to find his clothes and his dog covered in burdock burrs. After spending hours removing the unwanted burrs, he was curious to know how the burrs so easily clung to clothing, fur, and other objects.

He put one of the burrs under a microscope and discovered that its surface consisted of tiny hooks that could attach to any object that provided a receptive service. That receptive surface included anything that provided a loop, such as clothing, hair, or animal fur. De Mestral was struck by the burrs' exceptional sticking characteristics and pondered how to replicate them. After several experiments, he created a fabric that would function as a product fastener based on the burdock burr. He concocted a name for the material by combining the French words *velours* (velvet) and *crochet* (hooks) and called it Velcro.

NASA discovered that Velcro could secure pens, food packets, and other objects from floating away in space. Hospitals used it to affix blood pressure gauges to patient gowns. And *The New York Times* declared Velcro "The end of buttons, toggles, hooks, zippers, snaps, and even safety pins." In 1998, de Mestral made $93 million, and by 2012, Velcro was being sold in more than 40 countries. Even a simple moment of curiosity triggered by everyday frustrations can lead to revolutionary inventions that achieve global recognition and widespread success.

CHAPTER 22

Post-It Notes

Post-It Notes were always a self–advertising product because customers would put the notes on documents they sent to others, arousing the recipient's curiosity.

....

—Spencer Silver

Some of the best inventions have come when someone was curious enough to explore new ways to fix an issue. Sometimes, our attempt to fix a problem leads us to discover a different problem that we didn't know was a problem until we accidentally fixed it! Consider 3M designer Spencer Silver, who discovered Post-It Notes while he was trying to develop a strong adhesive. Initially, the adhesive he developed was weak, so he deemed it a failure. At the same time, another employee, Art Fry, needed to bookmark pages and found Silver's failed adhesive to be an excellent, reusable way to mark things. Together, the two men created Post-It Notes. Their curiosity and willingness to explore and experiment created this now-universal and ubiquitous product. By 2021, 600 Post-it Note products were being sold in more than 100 countries, and 3M sold more than 50 billion individual Notes that year.

While some have debated who created Post-it Notes, it might not surprise you that actress Lisa Kudrow did not. And although it was a running joke in the movie *Romy and Michele's High School Reunion* that they invented them, they did not. And while Alan Amron claimed to have invented the press-on memo a year before Post-It Notes were invented and filed suit against 3M (resulting in a confidential settlement), he did not. One thing is certain; when a great invention is discovered, everyone wants the credit.

CHAPTER 23

Monopoly

We were literally sitting around thinking, 'what would really corrupt Monopoly?' And someone said, 'what if we cheated?' Our senior marketer ... you could see him mulling it. Monopoly ... cheaters ... Cheater Edition! Hasbro instantly had the hook for a new game.

—Randy Klimpert

Sometimes, curiosity is about taking a fully-developed product and looking for new avenues to expand it. Most of us in the U.S. have played *Monopoly*. The company has done a fantastic job of developing different versions of its product based on customers' hobbies and interests, such as the cat or dog version. You may have even bought a *Star Wars* fan edition. Yet even with all those new versions, the makers of *Monopoly* wanted to come up with something even bigger and better—not just another version. They researched how people played *Monopoly* and discovered that more than half the people cheat when playing it (I'm sure none of you do that, right?). And because so many do cheat, the makers came out with *Monopoly:*

Cheater's Edition. In this version, players who successfully cheat are rewarded, while those caught red-handed are penalized. One of the more severe penalties is going to jail, a remnant of the original game but with a twist: attached to the new board is a toy handcuff that the offending player must wear. *Monopoly: Cheater's Edition* was the company's second-biggest release since the initial release of Monopoly.

CHAPTER 24

Bubble Wrap

Alfred Fielding and Marc Chavannes discovered that the air-filled bubbles within their textured wallpaper had incredible cushioning properties. This realization sparked their curiosity, and they began to experiment with different materials and designs to optimize the cushioning effect.

—Joseph Wille

Some of the most exciting—and fun—discoveries have emerged when someone was trying to create one thing only to create something completely unexpected. Such is the case of bubble wrap, created by engineers Alfred Fielding and his Swiss partner Marc Chavaness. The two were tinkering in Field's New Jersey garage in 1957 to create a new three-dimensional wall covering by sticking shower curtains together. The bubbles that happened to get trapped between the two curtains during the process created a unique texture.

Although the wallpaper they made never took off, it had other valuable properties, which the inventors capitalized on when they re-shifted their focus to protective packaging. Curiosity sparked their discovery of bubble wrap, which Sealed Air's product care division introduced in 1960 and that was later valued at more than $7 billion (in 2022).

It has been estimated that 240,000 miles of bubble wrap are produced each year in over 52 countries. Like plastic, bubble wrap is not biodegradable, but it can be recycled and, more importantly, played with for hours by both children and adults when they pop its bubbles!

PART V

IMPACT OF AI

One of the most intriguing questions I'm asked involves AI's possible impact on organizational structures. AI can automate routine tasks and thus eliminate some management layers, enabling organizations to possibly flatten their structure. If they go this route, they must weigh a flatter organization's downsides as well as its upsides. One downside is fewer promotion options for workers, but one upside is increased employee autonomy.

Because AI can process vast amounts of data, it can facilitate cross-functional activities in a matrix. In this way, AI tools can help teams work more collaboratively. AI can also improve communication because it improves connectivity within more networked structures. We will likely see traditional job roles shift to skill-centric approaches that need help from AI, which could yield more team flexibility and agility. With its access to real-time data, AI can improve data-driven decision-making. As organizations increasingly use AI, it will likely eliminate some positions and repetitive, task-oriented jobs, although critical thinking, creativity, and emotional intelligence will still be in demand—all of which AI has trouble mimicking.

AI will also likely affect traditional leadership roles. In response to the changes that AI will bring, leaders must grow their emotional intelligence, strategic thinking, and judgment. They will continue to focus on promoting good ethics, eliminating bias, resolving resistance to change, and managing talent and AI-driven uncertainty. Leaders may also need to monitor AI-related safety and privacy concerns.

By improving curiosity, leaders can enhance working with AI, resolving its difficulties while magnifying its strengths.

Curiosity allows individuals to embrace change and more freely seek growth so that they can view AI as less of a disruption and more of a learning opportunity. By increasing curiosity, leaders can better use AI recommendations to make informed decisions, especially those that concern ethics and bias. Curiosity—the catalyst for all innovation—will allow leaders to promote AI as an innovation source rather than as a threat. Curious leaders will encourage their teams to learn about and explore AI. Improving curiosity can also improve the emotional intelligence needed to voice any concerns about implementing AI.

* * *

Curiosity drives advancements in AI technologies like ChatGPT and helps shape the future of job security. Curiosity is not just a human trait; it is a force that propels AI's evolution and influences the job market. ChatGPT, a product of cutting-edge AI research, demonstrates curiosity's transformative power. Curiosity-driven exploration into how machines can understand and generate human-like text helped develop language models like ChatGPT. The result was a tool that can comprehend context, develop coherent responses, and adapt to various conversations.

Artificial curiosity, a concept within AI research, takes inspiration from human curiosity to enhance machine learning algorithms. Curiosity-driven AI systems actively seek novel information, explore uncharted territories, and adapt to evolving environments. This curiosity-driven approach improves AI models' learning capabilities and opens avenues for innovation across industries.

As we explore what it means to be curious about AI, one crucial issue arises: job security. AI's evolution prompts a fundamental shift in the job market, and individuals who remain curious about AI are well-positioned to navigate this transformation.

Understanding AI and its intricacies allows individuals to adapt and acquire new skills, aligning themselves with an evolving job market. Curiosity about AI fosters a proactive mindset, encouraging individuals to explore how AI can augment their roles, automate repetitive tasks, and create opportunities for higher-level skills development.

Curiosity about AI gives individuals the foresight to identify emerging job sectors and skill requirements, which in turn can empower them to make informed career decisions and stay resilient amidst technological disruptions. Workers and job-seekers who stay up-to-date on the latest AI developments are better positioned to contribute to, rather than be displaced by, the changing employment landscape.

CHAPTER 25

ChatGPT

In the realm of business, curiosity becomes the catalyst for innovation, transforming the interaction between user and ChatGPT into a dynamic partnership. Questions become the blueprint, and answers the building blocks, as this collaborative dance constructs a foundation for growth, where the inquisitiveness of entrepreneurs and the adaptive intelligence of ChatGPT converge to architect a future of endless possibilities.

—ChatGPT

Launched on November 30, 2022, ChatGPT is a chatbot developed by OpenAI. Based on a large language model (LLM), it enables users to refine and steer a conversation toward a desired length, format, style, level of detail, and language. Where Alexa and Siri provide information from the Internet, AI models like ChatGPT respond conversationally to users' queries with more coherent and relevant text.

Large language models like these can impact our curiosity and skills, and more attention and concern must be paid to this impact. *Fortune* magazine reported that the next era of work will center on skills rather than pedigree, and *The New York Times* reported that AI bots can write like Shakespeare *and* win art competitions. For some time now, many have worried about technology's impact on our curiosity and creativity. As long ago as 1995, the National Education Goals reported that curiosity was more predictive of later academic success than learning the alphabet or how to count.

Since 2006, I have taught business courses in higher education and have witnessed that when students have a knowledge gap, they need more curiosity and greater critical thinking skills. Curiosity fills that gap by generating new ideas. We must develop curiosity in our students and children if we want them, and our adult learners, to focus on thinking and problem-solving rather than worry only about getting the right answer. A 2022 study by the School of Education and Human Development at the University of Virginia observed 304 U.S. classrooms and found that instructors never asked their students to generate their own questions. Some books, like *Making Schools Work,* which presents data that supports curiosity's cultivation, have addressed how to help students develop curiosity through understanding how brains learn.

Like any technology, AI can be used for good or bad. We know that AI is going to improve, and Johns Hopkins experts advise educators to approach AI with curiosity. Parents and educators also need to explore AI with children. ChatGPT itself even displays curiosity whenever it asks clarifying questions when it isn't sure about the initial question it was asked.

Universities have included plagiarism and AI checkers to ensure students submit original content. However, such tools can't catch everything. It is so easy for students nowadays to type a question—often one directly from the course they are studying—into ChatGPT to obtain an instant answer. Students usually take that answer and paraphrase it to get around any anti-AI software their school is running. This is similar to a student lifting words or concepts from Wikipedia or a website and paraphrasing them.

What students don't realize is that the information on Wikipedia, websites, and ChatGPT is often unreliable. My courses require students to paraphrase citations from scholarly journals that they found in the school's library. However, like it or not, AI is here to stay and educators need to learn how to incorporate it. With that in mind, *The New York Times* reported that we should not ban AI but learn to teach with it. I agree that it is impossible to stop AI's progress; instead, we must embrace it and learn how best to use it while still encouraging curiosity-based exploration.

* * *

While the jury is still out regarding AI's impact on education, it has led many organizations to find success, and even thrive, thanks to AI-based programs. For example, Stitch Fix was founded in 2011 and leveraged AI algorithms to personalize clothing selections. Their system asks customers what they like or do not like and then adjusts the clothing sent based on their feedback. Customers receive highly personalized items inspired by a curiosity-driven culture that uses AI to help them improve their customers' experience. They continuously revise their AI algorithms based on customer feedback, which allows them to adapt to and compete in a changing retail market.

CHAPTER 26

Artificial Curiosity

AI is way more obsessed with learning than humans
are. Artificial curiosity is the exact opposite of human
curiosity; people are rarely curious about something
because they are told to be.

—Tomas Chamorro-Premuzic and Ben Taylor

When I wrote *Cracking the Curiosity Code*, I became interested in learning about artificial curiosity. At the time, there were studies where AI software programs were rewarded for discovering new things—and their curiosity could cost them. Sometimes, the software would let itself die in a game to see the Game Over screen or would flip through channels on the TV just to see something new. OpenAI explained that their algorithm would be rewarded for how wrong it was. At that time, they used games like Super Mario to teach curiosity because the game's object is to get to the next level. In Pathak and Agrawal's machine-learning version of this surprise-driven curiosity, the AI begins by mathematically representing what the current video frame of Super Mario Bros. looks like. It then predicts what the game will look like in several frames. The authors trained with intrinsic curiosity-based motivation (ICM). The system learned through repeated failures, eventually getting to the next level without being told to do so.

Whether with AI or people, too much curiosity can block decision-making. In order to thrive, both AI and humans need just the correct dose of curiosity. Therefore, researchers from MIT's Improbable AI Laboratory and Computer Science and Artificial Intelligence Laboratory (CSAIL) created an algorithm that overcomes the problem of AI being too curious and thus distracted by a given task. They tested this algorithm using over 60 video games. Their biggest challenge was to teach AI to discover useful information without getting off task, much like how a parent must help their child learn to manage its own curiosity.

In their *HBR* article, Tomas Chamorro-Premuzic and Ben Taylor asked if AI can ever become as curious as humans. They explained that curiosity is critical to developing talent and learning new skills, which in turn helps employees be more relevant at work. However, they also asked: What happens if AI becomes more obsessed with learning than humans, and how will that affect AI's desire to perform job-related tasks? Humans can self-direct their interests, but AI must be told what to be curious about. Computers have already surpassed humans in terms of task-related curiosity, but they struggle to make connections between unrelated experiences. Currently, artificial curiosity bridges the gap between human-like curiosity and algorithmic learning. However, humans still have the upper hand when it comes to discovering new, random things.

* * *

In addition to reaping other benefits from AI, organizations have used it to help create novel products, which required them to learn more about its capabilities. For instance, Alphabet's DeepMind has generated some of the most interesting AI research. Their curiosity-driven algorithms have explored new approaches to machine learning, and they attempt to create systems that learn more adaptively, much as humans do. Their AlphaGo creation made progress because it could adapt and learn to master a wide range of games without requiring programming. Their DeepMind healthcare initiative analyzes medical data and assists in diagnoses. By infusing curiosity into AI, organizations can adapt to various challenges, update algorithms based on feedback, and allow AI systems more autonomy while still adhering to ethical guidelines.

CHAPTER 27

Job Security

Pushing new frontiers in thought requires a deep curiosity that only humans are capable of—a curiosity cultivated by engaging in the works of great thinkers.

—John Manning, *Wall Street Journal*

In 1985, I worked in computer software sales. At that time, everyone was freaking out, worried that computers would eliminate jobs. Similar doomsday headlines still exist, this time speculating about how much AI (and technology) will replace jobs. Even creatives like writers and Hollywood actors are concerned that AI will soon do their jobs better and cheaper than they can.

Thankfully, not all AI predictions are pessimistic. AI can help people land jobs who could not previously do so. Consider non-native English speakers. MIT found that AI helped these job-seekers present themselves better on job applications, which improved their chance of being hired. And when they were hired, their employers were just as satisfied with these workers. AI can also improve brochures, presentations, white papers—the list goes on.

While computers have replaced some jobs since the 80s, they have also created new ones. The World Economic Forum stated that in 2025, 85 million jobs would be eliminated globally, but another 97 million new jobs would be generated. AI can match candidates to better jobs, which helps increase their chance of being hired (meaning they spend less time in dead-end interviews) and of finding fulfilling work.

In their 2023 research, Araz Zirar and Syed Imram Alie found that AI could potentially motivate employees (for more information, see "Worker and Workplace Artificial Intelligence (AI) coexistence: Emerging themes and research agenda, researchers" in the June 2023 issue of *Technovation*). However, AI does not always generate correct answers, and we still need humans to check and fix what AI produces.

For instance, Google's search algorithm mistakenly associated engineer Hristo Georgiev with a serial killer known as "The Sadist." The Robodebt scheme in Australia mistakenly issued 470,000 debts, which required the Australian prime minister to officially apologize and the government to issue a $1.2 billion settlement. Amazon's AI recruitment automatically incorporated gender bias, while Facebook's ads erroneously focused on protected characteristics and the UK Home Office's visa algorithm focused on nationality, which most considered racist. These issues underscore the necessity for a synergistic approach where humans and AI collaborate effectively.

If humans and AI must co-exist, allowing humans to work with AI will help uncover AI's limitations while empowering employees to explore new ideas. This coexistence will require training, which in turn will require organizations to ask what training is needed. These questions might include the following:

- What can AI do that humans cannot do in their organizations?
- What support can humans have to ensure AI does what is needed and intended?

Regardless of the answers to the above questions, human curiosity will continue to pave the way forward for successful organizations. For instance, Pymetrics has already used curiosity to provide personalized job matches for its customers. Founded in 2013, Pymetrics' neuroscience-based games align job-seekers with jobs based on the seekers' strengths, preferences, and abilities. Their game-like approach produces results that focus on abilities rather than (more traditional) resume-based criteria, which ultimately reduces bias and improves job satisfaction.

PART VI

PERSONAL IMPLICATIONS

Curiosity is a dynamic force that not only fuels passion but also shapes work experiences, influences work/life balance, and opens the door for growth. It ignites the passion at the heart of a fulfilling life. Individuals who are curious about their world are naturally inclined to explore, learn, and seek experiences that resonate with their interests. This curiosity-driven passion infuses life with meaning, purpose, and continuous wonder. Whether pursuing hobbies, traveling to unfamiliar places, or delving into diverse fields of knowledge, curious individuals live a passionate existence.

Curiosity can also help individuals align personal experiences with professional pursuits. Those who cultivate curiosity about their strengths, interests, and values tend to seek roles that resonate with them. This alignment enhances job satisfaction and fosters workplace purpose and fulfillment. Curiosity-driven individuals actively explore different facets of their professional identity, which integrates their experience with their work.

Curiosity guides individuals toward activities that bring joy and fulfillment, which is key to pursuing a balanced and meaningful life. Curious minds are more likely to engage in diverse experiences outside work, whether pursuing creative endeavors, connecting with nature, or deepening personal relationships. A curiosity-driven approach fosters a healthier work/life balance, ensuring that individuals find meaning and satisfaction in both their professional pursuits and in their personal life.

Opportunities for personal and professional growth abound for those who approach life with a curious mindset. Curiosity propels individuals to seek out challenges, acquire new skills, and embrace learning. In professional development, curiosity-driven individuals are more likely to grow, whether through continuous education, mentorship, or by exploring new career trajectories. Their willingness to ask questions, embrace uncertainty, and venture into uncharted territories will generate continued and expansive personal and professional growth.

CHAPTER 28

Passion for Life

Curiosity is the compass that leads us to our passions.
Follow it and you won't be disappointed. The future
belongs to the curious.

—Brian Grazer

I meet many people who would rather just exist than live a life of passion. They are stuck but often don't know that they are, and they have given up trying to find meaning. Regardless of what people do with their lives, those who do find meaning in life do so by utilizing curiosity.

Part of finding the right people, the right jobs, and the right passions in life includes searching for meaning and opportunities, which requires curiosity. When we are motivated internally and stoke our own curiosity, we are less likely to take only predictable actions. Instead, we learn how to solve problems and thus learn new skills that we can apply in work and in life. The first step to having a rewarding career is to ask what rewards us.

We have to try different things and not be afraid to explore and make discoveries. In his book *Range: Why Generalists*

Triumph in a Specialized World, journalist David Epstein shared how the more interests and experiences people have, the better they are at their jobs. According to Epstein, generalists, those with diverse interests and skills, tend to be more effective at doing their jobs and meeting new challenges than specialists. For instance, a ballerina might gain a different perspective and become a better ballerina if she also studies dance forms other than ballet. With range comes interdisciplinary thinking, learning from failure, and embracing a non-linear path to success.

If Steve Jobs had not followed his curiosity and taken a calligraphy course, we might not have the fonts we have today. After dropping out of college, he audited a course in Portland that taught him about typefaces, letter spacing, and creating designs. Years later, he used that knowledge to design the fonts for the Macintosh computer, and that detailed attention to fonts became the hallmark of Apple's design philosophy. By following his passion, Jobs inadvertently added a skill to his repertoire—one that changed history.

Steve Jobs is just one person who found meaning through exploration. Consider Leonardo da Vinci. His curiosity led him to observe, experiment, invent, and draw constantly. His work has continued to inspire people centuries after his death.

In 1955, Albert Einstein told *Time* magazine,

"The important thing is not to stop questioning. Curiosity has its own reason for existing. One cannot help but be in awe when he contemplates the mysteries of eternity, of life, of the marvelous structure of reality. It is enough if one tries merely to comprehend a little of this mystery every day."

Through that contemplation, Einstein found meaning in his work and in his personal life.

In the chapter about engagement, you learned about finding meaning in jobs through developing curiosity. The same principles apply outside of the workplace. Finding something engaging feels like play rather than work; no one has to talk you into it. That exploration, however, often requires courage. In the fear chapter, you will learn more about overcoming fear and other factors that inhibit curiosity. By overcoming fear, we can know what we like (and dislike) and avoid committing to activities or pursuits that do not enrich our lives.

CHAPTER 29

Alignment of Experience

Curiosity is a powerful catalyst for boosting career-and job-related meaningfulness.

—Alison Horstmeyer

Exploring our curiosity can align our expertise and preferences with job responsibilities and lead to rewarding careers. When I interviewed Olin Oedekoven, CEO of Peregrine, he told me he hired people he knew had talent, but only designed the job description once he knew what would really engage them. To him, the old way of posting a job description before finding the candidate was like trying to fit a square peg into a round hole. He did not believe in shaping and molding someone to fit into a pre-defined position. Instead, he approached people whose core values he shared, whom he respected, and who were passionate about their field.

He shared the story of Bill, who had worked in higher education accreditation for over fifteen years. He knew and respected Bill and his knowledge and expertise as well as how he worked with schools worldwide. When Bill came to Olin one day and asked if he had a vacancy, Olin said, "Not really."

"I'm looking for a job," said Bill.

"You're hired," said Olin.

"What am I going to do?" Bill said.

"I don't know, but we'll figure it out," said Olin.

They spent a couple of days figuring it out, with Olin asking Bill what he liked to do, what he was good at, and what he was passionate about.

Olin considered himself a disciple of Jim Collins, the author of *Good to Great*, which taught The Hedgehog Concept, which Olin often talked about because it applied to both organizations and individuals. The concept asks people these questions:

What are you passionate about? What can you be the best at? Can we find an economic incentive associated with that and try to find the intersection of those three concepts?

As part of that discussion, Olin and Bill developed the job title of 'director of strategic alliances', and so Bill started down that path. Over the years, he would grow relationships with their partners worldwide, and that position has evolved as his talents have been unlocked and recognized. Bill and Olin kept reshaping Bill's job description to align with his talents and capabilities, and Bill's position eventually evolved into 'director of business development', a position that didn't exist years ago. He performed marvelously.

Olin also shared with me the example of Clarice. At a conference, Olin approached her and was struck by her intelligence, enthusiasm, and background. Olin said,

"I don't suppose you're looking for a job; I have one for you."

"What job?" she laughed.

"I'm not sure, but I want you on the team," he said,

"Are you serious? What am I going to do?" she said,

"I'm not exactly sure, but it sounds like you're good in the areas of quality assurance," Olin said.

"I have a real passion for that," she said.

"Let's mold something together that aligns with you," Olin said.

She joined Olin's company and her contract evolved into a whole new position description.

We are often told to follow our passion. But following your curiosity can be even more rewarding. What if your passions change? What if you don't find your passion when you are young? Rich Karlgaard, author of *Late Bloomers: The Hidden Strengths of Learning and Succeeding at Your Own Pace*, explored the idea that success and fulfillment in life are not limited to early achievers. Karlgaard challenges the societal obsession with early success and argues that individuals who bloom later in life can bring unique qualities and strengths to their endeavors.

Sometimes, we follow what we think is our passion when our actual passion might be something else. If we focus instead on our curiosity, we avoid following our anger, resentment, or feeling of disrespect when we consider switching careers. Curiosity initiates the learning journey, and through learning one can stumble on one's true passion—and sometimes discover multiple passions! These may include pursuits that can provide income or just be enjoyed for their intrinsic value. When someone discovers that they have a multitude of interests, this can lead to new personal and professional experiences. While there is no definitive rulebook on uncovering your passion, there are guiding principles to pursuing passion to benefit your career, including choosing curiosity over passion and developing your skills.

CHAPTER 30

Work/Life Balance

Productive curiosity is a powerful tool to help you slow down and reflect, so you can solve business problems, build better relationships, and reduce stress.

—Elizabeth Grade Saunders

Work/life balance describes our attempt to balance our time and energy between professional and personal responsibilities. Others view it as the convenience of managing one's personal life during the workday without having to ask permission to take care of personal business or explain ourselves to others. As the traditional caretakers, women more often question how to maintain their sanity while handling both work and family responsibilities.

An article in *Yale Alumni Magazine* suggested that curiosity and conversations could be helpful in managing and understanding work/life balance. Some questions to be asked might include the following:

- How do you define work/life balance?
- Has that definition changed over your career? If so, how has it changed, and how did you find or maintain balance?

- How does finding balance jibe with staying competitive in your line of work?
- Can women have it all—find balance and stay at the top—and if so, how?
- What advice can you give younger women? What do we tell the next generation of women facing these same issues?
- What are the core values that drive your work/life balance?

While these are important questions, they leave the problem of solving them up to women. In her December 2010 TED talk, "Why We Have Too Few Women Leaders," Sheryl Sandberg noted that work/life balance greatly affects women's progress in leadership roles. She said that women face challenges when juggling professional and personal responsibilities and she highlighted those societal expectations and gender norms that often add more burdens. Sandberg called for a reevaluation of these expectations and encouraged men and women to share domestic duties more equitably. She also advocated fostering supportive workplace cultures and policies that would enable individuals, particularly women, to navigate their career paths without compromising their personal life.

In her article, "Why Women Still Can't Have It All," published in the July/August 2012 issue of *The Atlantic*, Anne-Marie Slaughter explored the challenges women face in achieving work/life balance, particularly in high-profile and demanding career positions. Slaughter shared her experiences as a professional and delved into the broader societal and structural issues that contribute to the struggle for balance. She argued that the prevailing work culture and expectations, often incompatible with the demands of family life, hinder women from attaining both professional success and personal fulfillment. Slaughter called for a reevaluation of workplace norms, policies, and societal attitudes in order to create a more inclusive environment that accommodates women's aspirations and complex lives.

Curiosity can help women seek a work/life balance, as it helps them explore new strategies and solutions to navigate and integrate their professional and personal aspirations. Curiosity fosters a learning mindset, and women and men striving to achieve a work/life balance can use curiosity to seek further information, learn from others' experiences, and adapt their approach to align with their personal and professional goals. Curiosity also encourages questioning and challenging existing norms.

Women who are curious about the societal expectations and workplace structures that hinder work/life balance may be more inclined to advocate for change and to challenge the status quo. Curiosity can drive individuals to explore innovative work practices. Women curious about optimizing their time and productivity may discover and implement novel ways to fulfill their professional responsibilities while still maintaining a healthy personal life.

Both Sandberg and Slaughter emphasize the importance of passion and skill-building. Curiosity can play a role in this by prompting women to explore areas of interest, acquire new skills, and align their passions with their professional pursuits to sustain a healthy work/life balance. Organizations can also foster a curiosity culture, one in which employees can explore flexible work arrangements, advocate for family-friendly policies, and spur initiatives that support work/life integration.

When applied to work/life balance challenges, curiosity can inspire women and men to question, learn, and innovate in their personal and professional lives, contributing to a more fulfilling and balanced existence.

CHAPTER 31

Opportunities for Growth

Curiosity is one of the great secrets of happiness.

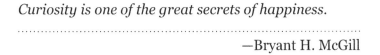

—Bryant H. McGill

One of the biggest mistakes leaders make is to try to keep their people from failing. That might sound like a good thing, but some of the most meaningful life and business lessons come through failure. Many project managers find questions stressful, and they fear getting off track. They don't recognize that when they limit questions and curiosity, they incur an opportunity cost. What issues might those questions have answered that could have shortened the process? When we are inflexible, we miss opportunities—even if those opportunities include potential failure.

After interviewing thousands of outstanding leaders on my radio show, I found that most, if not all, had experienced major failures that shaped their future success. Allowing people to fail safely is a skill that requires trust and the ability to enable people to see failure as an opportunity to learn. When failures occur, we should ask our employees to be curious about what went wrong and what they would do differently. We want them to fail smart and not fail the same way again.

You must be curious about what it will take to grow your career. This growth must stem from a personal choice and not from a command. Having a curious mindset to advance your career and expand your knowledge opens doors to countless opportunities. It empowers you to step beyond your comfort zone into uncharted territories and to accept fresh challenges. Embracing curiosity, being open to unfamiliar experiences, and welcoming new opportunities helps you acquire additional skills. In addition to spurring personal growth, curiosity contributes to a positive outlook and helps you make valuable connections on your journey.

Adopting a curious mindset also helps combat fears of the unknown, of failure, and even of success. Curiosity helps safeguard against falling into monotonous routines. Actively engaging in curiosity by exploring new knowledge and remaining receptive to daily possibilities helps banish boredom. Cultivating curiosity throughout one's life is the key to developing a lifelong attitude of learning. Because consistent daily learning is the cornerstone of both personal and professional advancement!

Psychologist Carol Dweck's mindset theory revolves around the concept of "fixed" and "growth" mindsets, where a fixed mindset assumes that abilities and intelligence are innate and unchangeable, whereas a growth mindset assumes and believes that abilities can be developed through dedication and hard work. Thus, people who adhere to a fixed mindset tend to avoid challenges, give up easily, see effort as fruitless, ignore helpful feedback, and feel threatened by others' success. On the other hand, those who follow a growth mindset encourage individuals to embrace challenges, persist in the face of setbacks, learn from criticism, and find lessons and inspiration in others' achievements. Dweck argues that cultivating a growth mindset leads to greater resilience, learning, and success.

Whether the story is about how Oprah Winfrey was fired or how Michael Jordan was cut from the team, there are countless examples of people who succeeded because they had grit—and curiosity leads to persistence behind grit. "Let's go invent for tomorrow rather than worrying about what happened yesterday," said Steve Jobs, who suffered through multiple failures, including being fired from Apple. "I didn't see it then," he said, "but it turned out that getting fired from Apple was the best thing that could have ever happened to me." Albert Einstein said, "We can't solve problems using the same thinking we used when we created them." We often hear about Einstein's successes, but he too had many failures, including failing the Swiss Federal Institute of Technology's entrance exam (he succeeded on his second attempt) and having his doctoral dissertation initially rejected for being irrelevant! Thomas Edison is often quoted as saying, "I have not failed. I have just found 10,000 ways that won't work." He didn't consider failure to be failure; for Edison, failure was feedback.

PART VII

EXAMPLES OF HIGHLY CURIOUS PEOPLE

Many prominent figures have harnessed the power of curiosity to achieve remarkable success. Consider Steve Jobs' creation of fonts and his exposure to calligraphy courses, Marie Curie's groundbreaking discoveries regarding radioactivity, Leonardo da Vinci's curiosity, which spanned art, anatomy, and engineering, and Jane Goodall's exploration of chimpanzees, which transformed our understanding of these beings and helped spur conservation efforts.

In the following chapters, I discuss five examples of curiosity's power, starting with Oprah Winfrey. Her innate curiosity about peoples' stories, combined with a desire to understand the human experience, fueled her amazing career. Thanks to her curiosity-driven approach, Oprah became a media mogul, connecting with millions and reshaping conversations on topics ranging from personal growth to larger social issues.

Warren Buffett, often regarded as one of the world's most successful investors, attributes much of his success to an insatiable curiosity about businesses. His voracious appetite for reading and learning about various industries enables him to make informed investment decisions. Buffett's curiosity-driven approach to understanding the intricacies of businesses has helped him become one of the world's wealthiest individuals.

Elon Musk's ventures into space exploration, electric vehicles, and renewable energy are fueled by his insatiable curiosity about the future of humanity. His relentless pursuit of knowledge and his desire to solve complex problems has led to transformative innovations, making Musk a visionary leader who continually pushes the boundaries of technology.

Mae Jemison, the first African American woman to travel in space, embodies the spirit of curiosity-driven exploration. Her journey to astronaut from physician, engineer, and entrepreneur reflects her deep curiosity about the world—and beyond. Jemison's multifaceted career exemplifies how curiosity can drive individuals to explore diverse fields and make significant contributions.

Albert Einstein's groundbreaking contributions to physics and to our understanding of space and time spring from his unyielding curiosity about the nature of reality. His thought experiments and persistent questioning of established theories helped him arrive at profound new insights. Though he earned the Nobel Prize in Physics for his discovery of the photoelectric effect, his discoveries about space and time changed the way we view reality. His childlike curiosity questioned the fundamental principles of the cosmos and propelled his genius.

CHAPTER 32

Oprah

Life was meant to be lived, and curiosity must be kept alive.

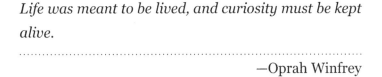

—Oprah Winfrey

Oprah Winfrey's insatiable curiosity and relentless pursuit of knowledge have propelled her success. Born into poverty to an unwed teenage mother in rural Mississippi, Oprah faced numerous challenges throughout her early life. However, her innate curiosity and determination to learn paved the way for her extraordinary journey to success.

In her teenage years, Oprah's curiosity found an outlet when she secured a job in radio broadcasting at WVOL, a local radio station in Nashville. Despite being a teenager, Oprah's innate ability to ask insightful questions and connect with people caught the attention of her audience. This early experience ignited her passion for media and storytelling.

Oprah's curiosity also drove her to excel academically, earning a scholarship to Tennessee State University. While attending college, she continued to explore her interest in media and worked at a local radio station, eventually becoming a television news reporter. Her curiosity delved deep into storytelling; Oprah sought to understand and empathize with those she interviewed and with their diverse stories and struggles.

In 1984, Oprah took a leap of faith and relocated to Baltimore to work as a news anchor. Unfortunately, hard news was not a good fit for her; her empathy and often spontaneous display of emotions did not jibe with her producers, who expected a smoother, more professional delivery. Still under an expensive contract, she was shunted off to fill lower-level positions at the station until she was recruited to host a morning talk show called *People Are Talking*. It was here that her innate curiosity and ability to connect with people truly shone. Oprah's genuine interest in her guests' stories and her empathetic interviewing style resonated with viewers; she and her skills had finally found their place. This success laid the foundation for her later move to Chicago, where in 1986 she launched *The Oprah Winfrey Show*.

What set Oprah apart was her drive to more deeply understand the human experience. She fearlessly tackled myriad topics, from personal development and mental health to social issues and spirituality. Oprah displayed her curiosity when she explored diverse perspectives and spoke openly about previously taboo subjects.

As *The Oprah Winfrey Show* gained worldwide popularity, Oprah's influence extended beyond television. Her curiosity led her to launch her own production company, Harpo Productions, and to later create the Oprah Winfrey Network (OWN). She continued to diversify her interests through various ventures, including book clubs, philanthropy, and acting.

Oprah Winfrey's journey exemplifies the transformative power of curiosity. Her ability to ask profound questions, explore diverse narratives, and connect with people on a genuine and profound level has made her into a media and social icon and has inspired millions. Oprah's story reinforces the notion that genuine curiosity, when coupled with hard work and determination, can generate unparalleled success.

* * *

Oprah has been very candid about her failures, for example her initial struggles to create her Oprah Winfrey Network (OWN) in the early 1990s. Known for her agility and curiosity, Oprah acknowledged the network's need for change. Thanks to a hands-on, curiosity-based approach, she learned her audience's preferences and explored programming that resonated with them. Oprah overhauled OWN in 2012 by bringing in new shows, documentaries, and interviews that appealed to her audience. She utilized her curiosity to revamp her network, and from her failure she learned to create an ultimate success. Her curiosity added to her resilience, and as always she used that curiosity to grow and flourish.

CHAPTER 33

Warren Buffett

Cultivate curiosity and strive to become a little wiser every day.

—Warren Buffett

One of the most successful investors of all time, Warren Buffett is known for his insatiable curiosity and lifelong commitment to learning. His story reflects how curiosity played a pivotal role in his path to success.

In the early 1950s, Buffett was working as an investment salesman. However, his true passion lay in understanding businesses and investing. His curiosity led him to explore the teachings of Benjamin Graham, a renowned economist and investor. Buffett was particularly drawn to Graham's value investing philosophy, which focused on finding undervalued stocks to invest in over the long term.

Buffett's curiosity didn't stop there. He went on to study at Columbia Business School under Graham, immersing himself in financial theories and investment strategies while also working for Graham's partnership.

What truly set Buffett apart was his relentless curiosity to understand the intricacies of businesses. Instead of relying solely on traditional financial metrics, he delved deep into company reports, industry dynamics, and management practices. He viewed holding stocks as owning part of a business, rather than owning a piece of paper.

Buffett's insatiable curiosity extended beyond finance. He read widely, studying economics and psychology, and drew insights from various other disciplines. His intellectual curiosity allowed him to connect seemingly unrelated fields and provided him with a unique investing perspective.

In 1962, Buffett began investing in Berkshire Hathaway, a struggling textile company, and in 1965 took control of it. The clothing business itself eventually failed, but he used his well-developed curiosity and business acumen to transform Berkshire into a holding company that became a powerful and diversified conglomerate. Under the Berkshire Hathaway name, he strategically invested in companies with strong fundamentals, long-term potential, and capable management.

Buffett's annual letters to shareholders became legendary for their clarity, wisdom, and investment insights, and he used these missives to share both financial lessons and his views on life and business.

Throughout his very long career—as of this writing, he's a few months shy of 94 and still working!—Warren Buffett's curiosity has propelled him to continuously adapt his investment strategies. He's never stopped learning and continues to embrace new technologies, industries, and economic changes.

His story illustrates how an inquisitive mind and a commitment to continuous learning can produce extraordinary success in the complex world of finance and business.

* * *

Not everything Warren Buffett attempted succeeded— even the greatest achievers make mistakes! However, when he shuttered Berkshire Hathaway's textile business in 1985 (he believed it was undervalued), his curiosity-driven approach helped him avoid clinging to status-quo ways and he redirected his capital to more lucrative holdings. Curiosity helped him discover his error and take what he'd learned to avoid making the same mistake. Thanks to his curiosity, Buffett learned to view failures as lessons on his long-term road to investment success, and his ability to pivot based on learning information has led to his enduring success.

CHAPTER 34

Elon Musk

I think curiosity is an extremely important thing to have. And [we need] to be somewhat obsessive about that curiosity.

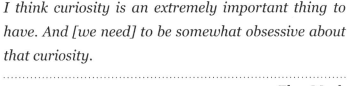

—Elon Musk

Elon Musk's insatiable curiosity and willingness to explore uncharted territories have played a pivotal role in his remarkable success, although many find some of his business (and personal) choices controversial, to say the least. Elon's curiosity-driven journey began in his childhood, during which he voraciously read books across various disciplines. This wide-ranging curiosity fueled his desire to understand complex topics and solve challenging problems. As a young boy in South Africa, he taught himself computer programming and developed a video game called Blastar.

Recognizing the Internet's potential, Musk ventured into the digital realm. In 1996, he co-founded Zip2, a city guide software for newspapers. Despite numerous challenges, Musk's curiosity and determination drove him to learn about the intricacies of the business world, from securing funding to managing a company.

After he sold Zip2, Musk founded X.com, an online payment company that later became PayPal. Once again, Musk delved into an unfamiliar industry, immersing himself in the complexities of finance and technology. PayPal's eventual success, which led eBay to acquire it, was a key milestone in Musk's entrepreneurial journey.

However, Musk's curiosity didn't stop there. He next turned his attention to aerospace, which is notorious for its challenges and its high financial and technological barriers to entry. In 2002, in order to make planetary exploration possible and affordable, he founded SpaceX. Musk's inquisitive mind and commitment to pushing boundaries led SpaceX to achieve such milestones as the creation of Falcon 1, the first privately developed liquid-fueled rocket to reach orbit.

Simultaneously, Musk set his sights on the automotive industry, an arena already dominated by well-established players. Musk created Tesla to revolutionize the electric car market by challenging industry norms and a prevailing skepticism. His curiosity-driven approach pushed technological boundaries, leading him to explore everything from electric vehicle design to battery technology.

Despite facing setbacks as well as skepticism from industry experts, Musk used his relentless curiosity and determination to help Tesla emerge as a major player in the automotive market, transforming our very notion of what an electric vehicle can be.

Musk's journey is a testament to curiosity's power to drive innovation and success. With his ability to pivot between industries and fueled by an insatiable desire to learn and solve complex problems, Elon Musk has become one of the most influential and successful entrepreneurs of our time.

* * *

Elon Musk's curiosity-driven approaches include iterative engineering, learning from each failure, and transparent communication when it comes to any necessary fixes. Although he faced many challenges with Tesla and PayPal, SpaceX provided him with some of his biggest ever. And though he could have easily given up after several failed attempts, instead he used those failures to make the necessary changes that finally led to his rocket's successful launch.

CHAPTER 35

Mae Jemison

Don't let anyone rob you of your imagination, your creativity, or your curiosity. It's your place in the world; it's your life. Go on and do all you can with it, and make it the life you want to live.

—Mae Jemison

Mae Jemison, the first African American woman to travel in space, exemplifies how curiosity and a passion for learning can drive remarkable success. From a young age, Jemison was curious about the world around her. Growing up in Chicago, she was fascinated by science, space, and the wonders of the universe. Her parents encouraged her inquisitive nature, providing her with books and resources to explore her interests.

Jemison's curiosity led her to pursue a scientific education. She earned a Bachelor of Science degree in Chemical Engineering from Stanford University and later a Doctor of Medicine degree from Cornell University. Her diverse educational background reflected her multidisciplinary curiosity, one that combined interests in both engineering and medicine.

Even while working as a general practitioner and conducting medical research, Jemison's fascination with space persisted. Driven by her belief that space exploration was an extension of human curiosity and a natural progression for scientific discovery, she applied to NASA's astronaut program. In 1987, Mae Jemison made history by becoming one of the 15 candidates selected out of a pool of over 2,000 applicants to join NASA's astronaut corps. Her journey showcases not only her exceptional academic and professional qualifications but also her unwavering curiosity and determination to explore the unknown.

On September 12, 1992, aboard the Space Shuttle Endeavor, Mae Jemison realized her childhood dream when she became the first African American woman in space. During her mission, she conducted scientific experiments in materials science, life sciences, and in human adaptation to weightlessness.

After leaving NASA, Jemison continued to pursue her wide-ranging interests as she worked in technology, education, and the arts. She founded the Jemison Group, a technology consulting firm, and she remains a strong advocate of STEM (Science, Technology, Engineering, and Mathematics) education.

Curiosity helped drive Mae Jemison's achievements. Her journey from curious child to pioneering astronaut and advocate for scientific education illustrates that nurturing one's curiosity can ultimately create opportunities that improve life for everyone.

* * *

Although Jemison's career has been remarkable, she was afraid of heights. Instead of focusing on her fear, however, she pushed ahead and viewed her fear as a weakness only if it kept her from doing what she wanted. And rather than focus on that weakness, she relied on her strengths in order to gain the upper hand. Like other curious achievers profiled in this book, Mae Jemison was not afraid to ask questions, and this led her to optimize her abilities and reach her goals.

CHAPTER 36

Albert Einstein

I have no special talents. I am only passionately curious.

....

—Albert Einstein

Arguably the most famous physicist in history, Albert Einstein attributed much of his success to his insatiable curiosity and relentless pursuit of knowledge.

In 1905, often referred to as his "miracle year," Einstein worked as a patent examiner in the Swiss Patent Office. In the evening and on weekends, however, he delved into theoretical physics. It was during this period that he developed his groundbreaking theory of special relativity.

Einstein's curiosity was sparked by one simple question: What if you could ride alongside a beam of light? This seemingly innocuous query led him to explore the nature of time, space, and the speed of light, and while delving deeper into this question, he formulated the famous equation $E=mc^2$ that revolutionized our understanding of energy and matter. But his curiosity didn't stop there; Einstein also explored the photoelectric effect and laid the foundation for quantum theory. And because of his openness to new ideas and his ability to challenge existing scientific paradigms, he was awarded the Nobel Prize in Physics in 1921.

Einstein's journey continued with his curiosity driving him to refine and expand his theories. He spent years developing his general theory of relativity, which predicted phenomena such as gravitational waves and the bending of light around massive objects.

Einstein's curiosity extended beyond physics. He was deeply engaged in societal and philosophical questions, and he advocated for civil rights, pacifism, and international cooperation. His curiosity about the universe and humanity's place in it fueled his passion for understanding not only the intricacies of physics but also the complexities of life itself.

In essence, Einstein's curiosity led to groundbreaking discoveries and reshaped the foundations of science. His willingness to explore the unknown, question established norms, and follow his curiosity is a testament to the transformative power of inquisitiveness when one pursues knowledge and innovation.

* * *

Just hearing the name Albert Einstein conjures images of both genius and success. However, even Einstein struggled in school. While his teachers balked at his rebellious nature and unconventional curiosity, he questioned their rigid teaching methods. Einstein even failed Zurich Polytechnic's entrance examination. But he persevered! He studied independently and used his curiosity to publish his groundbreaking discoveries. And despite his early scholastic struggles, he eventually became a worldwide symbol of the individualist who embraces curiosity to forge new scientific pathways.

PART VIII

EMBRACING THE STATUS QUO

Failing to embrace curiosity or to break free from status-quo thinking has proven detrimental to numerous organizations. From Theranos's lack of transparency and failure to question the feasibility of its claims to WeWork's decline due to a poor business model and overreliance on aggressive expansion, organizations that have clung to status-quo behaviors have failed.

Kmart failed to adapt to changing consumer preferences and embrace innovation, which led to its decline. The company stuck to traditional retail models and did not harness emerging technologies and e-commerce, which resulted in their losing significant market share.

Blockbuster ignored digital streaming and kept to their bricks-and-mortar rental model, which spelled its doom. Even as the market lurched toward online streaming, Blockbuster clung to the familiar and failed to see digital entertainment's potential.

Despite helping to pioneer digital photography, Kodak failed to fully capitalize on its invention. They failed to adapt and innovate when they refused to shift from their lucrative film business to digital photography. In the face of rapidly changing technology, Kodak's status-quo thinking spelled its decline.

Enron's spectacular collapse stemmed from a corporate culture that prioritized profits (achieved through financial manipulation) and ignored ethics. They failed to question and challenge dubious financial strategies and thus created one of history's most infamous corporate scandals.

Nokia and RIM BlackBerry, once dominant players in the mobile industry, needed to adapt to the smartphone revolution. Instead, they adhered to traditional mobile phone models and were reluctant to innovate in response to changing consumer demands, which enabled competitors like Apple and Android to grab much of their market share.

Polaroid failed to embrace digital photography, and this marked the end of an era for the iconic instant-photo company. Polaroid remained committed to its traditional film-based business model, which prevented it from capitalizing on emerging technologies and ultimately led to their bankruptcy.

Toys "R" Us struggled to adapt to the changing retail landscape and the rise of e-commerce. Because they failed to innovate their business model and connect with modern consumers, they eventually went bankrupt.

Once a pioneering force in aviation, Pan Am (Pan American World Airways) did not adapt to regulatory changes and shifting industry dynamics, leading to its decline. Their reluctance to diversify and innovate ultimately resulted in bankruptcy.

Lehman Brothers' demise during the 2008 financial crisis stemmed from risky financial practices and the organization's inability to question unsustainable investment strategies. Their failure to challenge the status quo in the financial industry contributed to one of the most significant collapses in banking history.

Once an early Internet trailblazer, Yahoo! faltered because it failed to innovate or adapt to the changing digital landscape. Their reluctance to embrace emerging trends and technologies contributed to Yahoo!'s diminished relevance.

The common thread here is that each company failed to foster curiosity within their culture and were reluctant to question established norms. Their inability to break free from status-quo thinking, adapt to changing environments, and embrace innovation ultimately led to their downfall.

CHAPTER 37

Kmart

The Kmart bankruptcy is a reflection of how the big discounters have lost their way. Kmart has lost its identity.

—Burt Flickinger III

Kmart was once a retail powerhouse offering a diverse range of products. One of the largest retailers in the United States at its peak in the late 1990s, Kmart had a market capitalization greater than $36 billion. But, as change swept through their industry, Kmart grappled with challenges that would eventually lead to its demise.

Formidable competitors like Walmart and Target rose to prominence because they mastered the art of contemporary shopping by providing competitive prices and modern, inviting stores. Unlike their competitors, Kmart failed to invest in technology, which hampered their supply chain management, leading to low inventory control and out-of-stock items. Kmart was unable to catch up with these evolving retail dynamics.

Over time, Kmart's physical stores began to show signs of

neglect. While their competitors invested heavily in store renovations, technological advancements, and overall improvements, Kmart failed to update their locations and so shoppers gradually beat a path to their competition's nicer stores. Kmart declared bankruptcy in 2002, marking one of the most significant filings in the history of retail.

Had they built a culture of curiosity, Kmart could have asked why Walmart and Target were more successful in adapting to changing consumer desires and trends. They could have researched how better to invest in updated stores, technology, and infrastructure. They could have created a plan to manage and address supply chain issues and improved customer satisfaction by asking shoppers what they really wanted from Kmart's stores.

However, because of their status-quo thinking, they failed to embrace e-commerce and shifting consumer behaviors. Their business died because they failed to adapt and promote a new customer experience. In short, stiff competition, strategic missteps, financial troubles, and Kmart's inability to adapt to changing consumer preferences contributed to their demise.

CHAPTER 38

Blockbuster

Netflix was never meant to be the demise of Block-buster. It was the evolution of the way people watch content. That was the demise of Blockbuster.

—Jim Keyes, Blockbuster CEO

At its peak, Blockbuster had a market value of around $5 billion. Much has been written about Blockbuster's demise, with many blaming them for missing the opportunity that Reed Hastings presented to them in the early 2000s. As the story goes, Hastings approached Blockbuster, the leading video rental chain at the time, and proposed a partnership. He suggested that Netflix could manage Blockbuster's online component, essentially becoming Blockbuster's digital arm.

Blockbuster was not the first to decline what they thought was probably just a passing niche market opportunity. Focused as they were on their brick-and-mortar stores, they did not see the offer's potential. They fell back on what had always worked for them rather than question where videos were headed. Eventually, Netflix added streaming, which allowed them to reach an even broader audience and become a major entertainment industry player. Netflix became synonymous with on-demand streaming. By the time Blockbuster saw where the industry was headed, however, it was too late. Blockbuster filed for bankruptcy in 2010, while Netflix's market capitalization had reached $250 billion by 2020.

Had Blockbuster questioned their market's direction and how they could improve their customers' experience, they might have saved their once-dominant company. Additionally, they underestimated the market and opened unneeded stores. All of the above, combined with their late entry into the digital market and failure to innovate, cost them dearly. Had they been more curious, asked more questions and created a strategic vision, they might have jettisoned their outdated business model and experienced a happier, Hollywood ending.

CHAPTER 39

Kodak

*Kodak did a good job of seeing the future; they just
didn't do a good job of getting there.*

—John Kotter

When I was a kid, I could not walk into a store without
running into a display of Kodak products. Their name was synonymous with photography. They pioneered innovations in film
and cameras and seemed too big to fail. At its peak in the late
1990s, Kodak's market capitalization was around $30 billion.
Once an industry titan, Kodak failed to recognize the power of
digital transformation, ultimately leading to its downfall.

Their fatal mistake came when they hesitated to embrace
digital imaging. Heavily invested in film and print, they worried
that digital imaging would cannibalize their lucrative film sales.
Like Blockbuster, they clung to past successes and missed where
consumers were headed. By the time they got on board the digital
bandwagon, they were no longer the dominant player.

In 2012, Kodak, a company that once held a near-monop-
oly on photographic products, filed for bankruptcy. They might

have avoided this fate had they been more curious and looked at digital photography from a consumer perspective. They could have pivoted quickly and recognized that their pre-existent model included high fixed costs. Any organization that clings to outdated models and relies on status-quo behaviors loses adaptability, which is the key to survival.

CHAPTER 40

Enron

Enron is a stark reminder of the perils of high-stakes innovation without proper oversight and accountability.

—Bethany McLean

At its peak, Enron, an energy company, was worth around $70 billion. On the surface, Enron was too big to fail. However, executives Jeffrey Skilling and Ken Lay had creatively hidden debts and losses to paint a glowing organizational picture that artificially propped up stock prices and kept them soaring. They also bet heavily on energy derivatives (while hiding their downside), which resulted in further losses. In 2001, their house of cards fell and they filed for bankruptcy, making them one of the most significant corporate scandals in history.

One of my favorite guests on my radio show was Bethany McLean. In 2001, she published an article on Enron in *Fortune* titled "Is Enron Overpriced?" In it she suggested that something unusual had happened with their financial documents. She later wrote the book *The Smartest Guys in the Room*, which detailed Enron's corrupt business practices. When I asked her how curiosity played into her success in discovering what happened at Enron, she told me this:

"Twenty-plus years of working as a journalist has made me much more engaged and curious than I was. Part of that is to figure things out. I can come up with ideas I don't understand, and I have the forum to work on them and think about them. It goes back to this notion that you shape yourself by how and where you spend your time and who you spend time with."

She had to figure out why what she saw happening at Enron did not correspond to what they reported was happening.

Enron might have avoided some of the factors contributing to their downfall if they had embraced a culture of curiosity. For starters, they should have explored their leaders' ethics—or lack thereof. After Enron collapsed, many employees lost not only their jobs but their entire retirement savings as well, since many had invested mostly in Enron's now-worthless stock. (Hint: avoid investing heavily in your company's stock, because if your company fails, you will lose your job *and* your life savings.) Had more Enron employees been curious about what would happen if the company were to crash, maybe fewer lives would have been shattered. In the end, the Enron scandal prompted regulatory reforms and increased scrutiny to prevent similar failures.

CHAPTER 41

Nokia

Nokia in a sense is a victim of its own success. It stayed with its playbook too long and didn't change with the times.

—Jyrki Ali-Yrkkö

Nokia was once *the* dominant force in the mobile phone industry. At their peak in 2000, they were valued at around $300 billion. Their inability to adapt to the smartphone era eventually allowed Apple and Samsung to eclipse them. Nokia attempted to cling to its market dominance by clinging to status-quo ways, and in doing so they failed to consider the impact of smartphones. Nokia dismissed the iPhone's popularity, which proved fatal.

Nokia should have been curious about emerging trends, consumer preferences, and technological shifts. By the time they were, they were too far behind. In 2011, Nokia partnered with Microsoft to produce their smartphone, but it was not enough to save them. In 2014, they sold their devices and services division to Microsoft for $7.2 billion, which marked their exit from the smartphone industry and their shift to network infrastructure. Their pivot led to their significant role in developing 5G technology.

Nokia's lack of curiosity led them to stop innovating. They chose something called the Symbian operating system, which could have proved a more effective OS, but they missed out on touchscreen technology. Unlike Apple and Google, they failed to build an app ecosystem and were slow to adapt while facing stiff competition. Nokia's lack of curiosity and reluctance to embrace innovation resulted in their missing critical technological shifts, rendering them unable to compete effectively with pioneers in the fast-paced tech landscape.

CHAPTER 42

RIM BlackBerry

BlackBerry's failure to innovate and adapt to the rapidly changing smartphone landscape is a classic case study in the dangers of complacency in the tech industry.

—Jack Gold

There was a time in the mid-2000s when Research in Motion's (RIM) BlackBerry device was so ubiquitous and, apparently, addictive that some called it the CrackBerry. RIM's Black-Berry success peaked in 2008 when its market capitalization was around $83 billion. When Apple's and Google's phones became popular in the late 2000s, BlackBerry's lack of touchscreen and app ecosystem put it several steps behind its competition. And then in 2011 BlackBerry experienced a widespread outage, which damaged its reputation for reliability. By 2015, they recognized they could not compete in the hardware market and shifted to software services. By 2017, RIM fully shifted to providing technologies that ensure the safety and security of devices.

RIM's lack of curiosity and adaptability in the face of emerging trends ultimately led to the company's problems. They clung to iconic physical keyboards and failed to explore changing consumer preferences, which caused their downfall. They could have sustained their relevance and competitiveness had they explored their consumers' evolving needs and fostered a culture of curiosity to adapt to the changing landscape. Their lack of adaptability, resistance to change, and failure to introduce new features, combined with intense competition, a limited app ecosystem, and their delay in updating their OS, contributed to their failure.

They could have developed a more robust ecosystem had they been curious about touchscreen technology and invested in app development, an innovation that would have required opening up their platform to third-party developers. They also should have been more agile in making decisions, forming strategic alliances, integrating user feedback, and diversifying their product portfolio. Instead, they relied only on what had worked in the past and weren't curious about how to achieve long-term success in the technology industry.

CHAPTER 43

Polaroid

Polaroid's fall from grace is a story of missed opportunities and the failure to adapt to the digital age.

—Christopher Bonanos

When I was growing up, Polaroid was the epitome of an innovative company that produced an innovative product. Before Polaroid, it took what seemed like an eternity to get photos developed. Then Polaroid entered the picture and photography changed. Polaroid's ability to produce a photo almost instantaneously was exciting. The quality wasn't quite up to that of traditional film cameras, but we didn't care because we had something in our hands that we didn't have to wait for.

Founded in 1947, Polaroid was the brainchild of Edwin Land. The company dominated the instant picture market up until digital photography emerged and its capitalization peaked in 1980 at $3 billion. By the early 2000s, however, Polaroid had failed to adapt and by 2001 had filed for bankruptcy. They had high debt and declining sales, and they had failed to innovate and join the digital era, which caused them to lose customers and market share. They attempted a relaunch in 2008, experienced multiple ownership changes, and continued to need help with innovation. As of 2023, they have survived by innovating and introducing pocket-sized cameras that fit a niche market. Curiosity could have helped Polaroid recognize that the convenience their cameras offered could now be had with digital photography. In hindsight, Polaroid should have transitioned faster to digital photography and pursued strategic partnerships. Additionally, had they focused on continuous innovation and built a robust digital ecosystem (instead of relying only on physical instant prints), they would have responded better to changes in the market. They also failed in their brand and financial management and did not invest in communicating the benefits of their products.

CHAPTER 44

Toys "R" Us

Toys 'R' Us succumbed to the pressures of the digital age and shifting consumer behavior.

—Greg Melich

There are not many activities I enjoy more than going to a toy store. At its peak in 1998, Toys "R" Us was a major toy retailer valued at over $12 billion. By 2017, however, the company had filed for bankruptcy. In its heyday, it offered an extensive selection of toys and a fun shopping experience. However, their failure to embrace innovation and adapt to e-commerce led to their demise.

Had they utilized curiosity, Toys "R" Us would have learned more about what their customers wanted during their in-store experience. Curiosity also could have helped the company improve their supply chain's efficiency and helped them price their products more competitively, which is key to attracting more cost-conscious customers. Toys "R" Us could have researched point-of-sale technology, valued data analytics, and utilized target marketing—but they did none of these. They could have diversified and expanded their product base and done the same to their customer base to make it more global, and this might have sustained them.

After filing for bankruptcy, they closed stores and attempted to revitalize their brand. By 2018, they had created liquidation plans. Investors have acquired the brand and are trying to revive it by adding e-commerce platforms and Toys "R" Us locations inside Macy's department store. As of 2023, they operate stores at airports and on cruise ships, but their market share is not what it was.

CHAPTER 45

Pan Am

Pan Am's demise is a tale of a once-glorious airline that failed to adapt to the changing dynamics of the aviation industry.

—Jeff Kriendler, Former VP
Communications at Pan Am

Pan American World Airways (Pan Am) was once considered an innovative airline. In the early 1970s, their value peaked at $300 million. One of their biggest missteps came when they failed to embrace jumbo jets. Like their competitors, they struggled with high fuel prices and economic downturns, which lowered travel demands. Additionally, the 1988 Lockerbie Scotland terrorist attack, which resulted in 270 fatalities, targeted a Pan Am flight and eroded consumer confidence in the airline's safety. With too many unprofitable routes, intense competition, and poor leadership during and after the Lockerbie crisis, the airline needed to adapt to a dynamic industry. They ignored emerging technologies and became saddled with debt, filing for bankruptcy in 1991.

While it is challenging for any organization to come back from a terrorist attack, other companies have handled such crises better than Pan Am did. Consider the case of Johnson & Johnson and how they dealt with the cyanide poisoning of Tylenol, which killed seven people, including a 12-year-old girl. The Tylenol case is often cited as the gold standard in crisis management, showcasing how a well-executed response can save a company from disaster.

Pan Am's response to the Lockerbie bombing was slow, whereas J&J responded to the poisoning swiftly. Pan Am displayed poor communication and poor crisis preparedness, while J&J followed a well-established crisis management plan and took immediate responsibility for the incident, assuring customers of their commitment to safety. Had Pan Am utilized curiosity and thought ahead to create an effective communication and crisis plan and then followed it, their final outcome might have been different.

CHAPTER 46

Lehman Brothers

Lehman Brothers' downfall can be attributed to a toxic combination of excessive leverage, poor risk management, and exposure to subprime mortgage securities. The firm's overreliance on short-term borrowing and complex financial instruments amplified its vulnerability when the housing market collapsed, ultimately leading to its historic bankruptcy.

—Andrew Ross Sorkin

I worked in the mortgage industry in the early 2000s and I remember seeing loans get approved that never should have. At the time, applicants could "state" their income and borrow to buy a home despite poor credit and/or insufficient income. The industry called these subprime mortgages. While some of these borrowers were given conventional 30-year and 15-year loans, many opted for adjustable-rate mortgage (ARM) loans, whose interest rates were initially competitive but could adjust higher— much higher. The prevailing opinion was that the real estate market would continue to go up, giving subprime borrowers time to repair their credit and refinance their ARM before it *might* adjust higher. One friend I know was told by his mortgage loan officer, "It doesn't matter if your ARM's rate goes up; most people don't stay in their homes for more than seven years. And by then you probably will have moved to another house."

Of course, we now know that everything the mortgage industry said couldn't happen did happen; the economy slowed a little, over-inflated housing prices started to fall, and large numbers of subprime borrowers began to default on their loans because they were unable to pay their new, higher mortgage payment on a house that was now worth less than the outstanding loan. As a result, the mortgage-backed securities that investment banks had constructed by packaging together these bad loans became worthless, which brought down Lehman Brothers, one of the world's oldest and largest investment banks, helping to trigger the 2008 global financial crisis.

Prior to their downfall, Lehman Brothers was a mighty investment bank. At their peak in 2007, they were valued at over $600 billion. Lacking risk mitigation techniques, they invested heavily in mortgage-backed securities because they underestimated how risky these securities could be. Over-leveraged in an investment vehicle comprised mostly of risky subprime mortgages, Lehman Brothers became a ticking time bomb. When these securities began to fail, Lehman lacked the liquidity to cover their margins. Unable to meet their obligations, their credit rating declined and their creditors began to call in their debts. Market panic and loss of confidence led to their eventual demise as well as to that of other financial institutions exposed to Lehman. In September 2008, Lehman Brothers filed for bankruptcy.

A culture of curiosity could have helped them recognize that they were too heavily leveraged on subprime mortgages and would have enabled them to spread their risk, hedge their investments, or choose a different investment vehicle. In order to stabilize the financial markets, the federal government eventually stepped in and used taxpayer money to bail out many faltering institutions. By then, however, it was too late for Lehman Brothers.

CHAPTER 47

Yahoo!

Yahoo!'s decline can be attributed to a series of strategic missteps, internal turmoil, and an inability to keep pace with the rapidly evolving tech landscape. The failure to capitalize on emerging trends like search and social, coupled with leadership changes and missed acquisition opportunities, contributed to the erosion of its once-dominant position in the digital space.

—Nicholas Carlson

Yahoo! was *the* dominant search engine in the early days of the Internet. At its peak, it was valued at around $125 billion. However, they failed to recognize the power of emerging competitors like Google and it cost them dearly. Yahoo! missed the opportunity to keep pace as the Internet shifted toward user-generated content and social media. In 2017, they were acquired by Verizon.

Yahoo! lacked curious leadership. They should have explored innovation. Instead, they went through multiple CEOs and strategies, but what they needed was a more unified approach. And when in 2014 they suffered a significant security breach, people lost trust in their site's security.

The rise of Google and Facebook sealed their fate. From that point forward, Yahoo! struggled to sell online advertising and made high-profile acquisitions that did not pan out. Its brand lost its luster as shifts in user behavior exacerbated the company's financial struggles and contributed to its slow decline.

Yahoo! could have remained the dominant player had they capitalized on the emerging opportunities in search and advertising, maintained a stable leadership, innovated, and dealt more effectively with security breaches. In the end, however, their inability to embrace curiosity, the driving force of innovation and adaptability, led to their demise.

PART IX

HOW TO FIX IT

CHAPTER 48

FATE

You are the master of your fate, the captain of your soul.

....

—W.E. Henley

Numerous companies, such as Kodak and Blockbuster, once appeared to be destined to stand the test of time; however, they have now faded into history. In the era of artificial intelligence, organizations must embrace innovative ideas to avoid a similar fate. The challenge is to get an organization's culture to embrace curiosity. Can employees play a crucial role in this? If so, what might hinder them from being creative and motivated to offer their valuable perspectives and opinions?

If employees are an organization's greatest asset, they must nurture and cultivate their employees' innate curiosity. A thriving environment requires individuals who pose challenging or unconventional questions, venture into uncharted territories of ideas, and willingly embrace the unknown.

Although it's widely recognized that curiosity often declines with age, no one has yet identified why this happens. This prompted me to research the factors that inhibit curiosity. After all, before we can address and fix something, we must first understand why it's broken.

After studying thousands of people for many years, I determined that four factors inhibit curiosity, which I've represented with the acronym FATE (to help make it easier to remember). FATE stands for Fear, Assumptions, Technology, and Environment.

Consider the impact of fear. People avoid exploring new areas or asking questions because they fear failure, embarrassment, or losing control. I once asked a boss how to do something. Instead of offering guidance, he was mortified that no one had yet trained me to do that task and just said, "I'm going to pretend I didn't hear that." After hearing his reaction, I made sure never to ask him anything ever again. When leaders react in hostile, dismissive or offensive ways to simple, honest questions, their employees shut down.

Many leaders might not be aware that their reactions seem negative. When I confronted that leader about his behavior, he was utterly unaware of his comment's impact. Leaders like him are why emotional intelligence has become an essential workplace topic. If we fail to develop our empathy and interpersonal skills, our people will be afraid to ask us questions.

When we look at the second FATE factor, assumptions, we sometimes assume that something won't be interesting, exciting, or useful enough to warrant our interest. People often avoid pursuing things that they didn't like in the past or because someone they knew did not like it. As we age, however, past dislikes can often turn into likes because we have gained more experience. I remember trying to stay awake in my World History classes in school. There I learned about Pearl Harbor, but if someone had asked me then if that topic interested me, I would have said no. Later, after traveling to Hawaii and seeing the bombing's horrific aftermath firsthand, history came alive and became far more interesting to me. Many of us miss opportunities to learn new things because we tell ourselves that we won't be interested. Recognizing that we often sabotage our own learning and growth can help us work to develop our curiosity.

The third FATE factor that can inhibit us is technology. Sometimes, technology does so much for us that it keeps us from looking into how the answers were discovered. Technology can be so overwhelming that our thinking shuts down so that we fail to learn when presented with new opportunities. A big first step to get people to embrace their possibilities (so that they don't fall behind) is for companies to train their people in the relevant technologies.

The last FATE factor is the environment. Our environment includes family, educators, work relationships, peers, friends, social media, and just about everyone we come in contact with. When those around us don't have time to answer our questions or have ideas about what we should or should not do with our lives, our desire to ask questions and explore new opportunities can weaken. Peoples' desire to fit in can kill many dreams.

As you read about these four factors, consider how they have impacted your curiosity *and* how you affect others' curiosity as well. Whether we are parents, teachers, friends, co-workers, or leaders, we affect those around us. As we understand these FATE factors, we can improve our curiosity and help others be more curious as well.

If we examine these four areas within our lives, consider the worlds that can open up for us. If we no longer fear that our questions or ideas will be mocked or dismissed, if we no longer assume that something isn't interesting, if we embrace technology and its possibilities, and if we overcome the environmental influences that have held us back, what will that workplace look like? It will be one filled with workers who are engaged and excited, who come up with innovative ideas that disrupt the old ways, and who make organizations more productive.

We should never let FATE hold us back.

CHAPTER 49

Curiosity Code Index

Anyone who stops learning is old, whether at twenty or eighty.

—Henry Ford

Let me begin by saying that this is not a sales pitch for my assessment—as terrific as it is. I am including this information mainly because I think it can benefit trainers and HR professionals.

When I began researching *Cracking the Curiosity Code*, I was stunned to learn that no assessment yet existed to determine what inhibits curiosity. Some assessments determined curiosity levels, which was helpful, but first I needed to know what hinders curiosity to learn how to fix it. Because I had worked with emotional intelligence assessments during my doctoral research, I knew that personality traits and behaviors can be quantified. Therefore, I decided to create the Curiosity Code Index (CCI), the first and only assessment that determines the factors that *inhibit* curiosity.

I began by posting a survey within a LinkedIn business group to understand the barriers people face in being curious.

The responses overwhelmingly highlighted various facets of fear, prompting me to delve deeper into the complexity of curiosity inhibitors. Seeking assistance from statisticians and factor analysis experts, I strived to create an assessment to uncover the factors hindering curiosity. Despite several attempts, my results kept circling back to the same kind of results other assessments had already measured and logged.

Still determined to create an assessment that discovered what inhibited curiosity, I learned how to create assessments and perform factor analysis. Doing this unveiled four factors that could impede curiosity, factors that form the acronym FATE: fear, assumptions, technology, and environment.

I wanted my assessment to be more than just a lighthearted quiz on my website. For those interested in the nitty-gritty of research, I have published the Curiosity Code Index's validation in a scholarly, peer-reviewed journal.

For those eager to take the Curiosity Code Index (CCI), it's accessible at curiositycode.com. The assessment, which comprises 36 statements that require responses ranging from strongly agree to strongly disagree, takes about 10 minutes to complete and instantly generates a comprehensive report.

As individuals understand better how fear impacts curiosity, they learn how to deal with failure, embarrassment, and a loss of control. Other issues like competition, pressure, rejection, and expectations can also impact fear. Depending on their assessment results, people receive an action plan to help them resolve each issue identified. This essential action plan includes goals, timeframes, potential outcomes, threats, and support system options.

If you're not sure what I mean by assumptions, one example might be assuming that certain subjects are always boring, so you avoid reading about them. However, as individuals learn how assumptions can negatively impact curiosity, they often discover subtle factors that can inhibit their willingness to explore or be curious. When individuals uncover their assumptions—such as issues or topics they dislike now because they once disliked them, or areas they believe they have already sufficiently explored—they can then discover how those assumptions have either overtly or covertly curtailed or blocked their curiosity.

Technology can overwhelm people with the avalanche of information it generates. Individuals either believe that Siri, Alexa, or AI can already answer any and every question, or they feel overwhelmed by technology's onslaught. They may also resist the inevitable changes that accompany new technologies. Whatever technology's effect on someone, the CCI can help them better understand it—and themselves.

Lastly, our environment—particularly the people around us—can severely impact our choices. For example, one's family members can make you feel uncomfortable when your interests do not align with theirs. The CCI assesses this fourth and final factor, which is the degree that parents, college professors, pastors, siblings, friends, or influential people can negatively impact and inhibit our curiosity. It may be our culture. It may be our boss. Regardless of by whom or to what extent we are affected, the CCI assesses our environment's impact on our curiosity.

Even if you have not yet taken the assessment, the following chapters can help you improve in these four areas. Usually, someone would need to take the assessment and/or certification training to learn more about the CCI. However, these chapters on FATE provide much of the information I share in my training courses.

* * *

Because I can't be everywhere and meet with everyone, I train HR professionals and consultants to administer the CCI. Many organizations have provided personality assessments such as emotional intelligence, DiSC, and engagement surveys. Unlike a DiSC or MBTI (Myers Briggs) assessment, however, the CCI does not categorize people. It provides a baseline measurement of the factors that inhibit their curiosity. The CCI is much like an emotional intelligence assessment because its results identify levels rather than place people into categories. Through taking the CCI, individuals learn how much these factors affect them and then receive instructions on how best to overcome these issues.

Leaders often have concerns about innovation. They recognize that technology, including AI, robotics, etc., will replace some human jobs and responsibilities. Thus, it's more important than ever to ensure that employees are trained to assume new and different tasks and even entire jobs. Hence it is essential to ensure that work responsibilities match each person. Allowing people to develop their natural curiosity can open the door to new job responsibilities and opportunities and spur them to make new discoveries about themselves. Aligning people with jobs that spark their curiosity can help improve their engagement.

Innovative leaders understand that creating a culture of curiosity requires that they embrace change as well. Leaders who welcome this change employ leadership consultants to either train HR staff to administer the CCI to their employees, or have the consultants administer it directly to employees. Either way, the CCI training takes around a half day. Based on the results obtained in the training, leaders and consultants then determine how much time to spend on follow-up training.

The CCI training has two outcomes. The first is that individuals receive their confidential CCI scores and create an action plan for overcoming the factors that negatively impacted their curiosity. The second is that trainees, as a group, help create action items and plans to overcome the problems the organization has experienced.

Prior to training, CCI-certified experts discuss the top issues that leadership believes are problematic and then explain what issues employees feel are problematic during the exercise. Having now learned the importance of curiosity, employees then address those issues and factors that have impacted them and then create action items to give to the consultant or HR professional, who then presents a report to leadership based on that feedback.

For example, if leaders find that critical thinking is problematic, after the assessment, employees would create a task to help them develop their curiosity and become better critical thinkers. An example of a task might be to allow employees to present a topic of their choice at a weekly meeting, which could include how to better perform a given task. This could require the employee to be a subject matter expert and explain an area that interests them and that they want to know more about. Because there is no better way to learn something than to teach it, the employee should pick something that appeals to their interest and that requires research to allow them to learn more about the subject and how best to present it.

CCI training given to HR professionals certifies them to provide CCI training to the organization and gives them SHRM recertification credit. As mentioned previously, an out-side-trained CCI consultant can also train the employees directly if a company lacks an HR department or prefers to use a consultant.

When I train groups of consultants and HR professionals, I love to watch their expressions when they recognize the factors that have inhibited them. They always have an "Aha!" moment that encourages them to ask questions. And isn't that the point? The first exercise, where they complete the personal goals and strategies, gives them the insight to provide great input for the second part, which is about giving feedback to leaders.

When leaders provide me with their issues prior to training, these often include concerns about communication or innovation, much like Disney's issues regarding how to improve their internal laundry service (see Chapter 14). The employees, now armed with the knowledge of how to fix their personal problems with curiosity, can utilize what they have learned to provide beneficial feedback to leaders regarding issues these have brought up.

After the trainer writes their summary report, leaders can use that information to make changes the way Disney did. As you may recall, by asking just one question, Disney garnered more than $100,000 in savings. Imagine the benefit that feedback regarding cultural issues can have on organizations willing to go through these assessments and exercises.

* * *

When I begin the CCI training programs, I give an overview of curiosity and why it is essential, and I include research, stories from top thought leaders, and positive organizational outcomes.

I often share a thought experiment that demonstrates how people go along with status-quo thinking. To prove this point, a hidden camera was set up in an eye doctor's office. A woman went into a doctor's office thinking she was getting an eye exam, but she was really part of the experiment. Although she believed the people in the waiting room were patients, they were all actors. While they sat there, waiting to get called back to see the "doctor," a bell would ring every few minutes.

Every time that bell rang, all the actors around her, who she thought were patients, would stand up and sit down without explanation. After hearing the bell ring just three times and without knowing why she was doing it, the woman stood up and sat down, conforming with the group.

Seeing that she went along with what everyone else did, the researchers then wanted to see what would happen if they took everybody out of the room but still rang the bell. So, they called everybody back one at a time as if they were patients, leaving the woman alone in the room. And when the bell rang again, she again stood up and sat down. She obviously didn't know why she was doing it, but she went along because it was what everyone else had done.

The researchers then added some real patients to the room to see both how they and the woman would respond when the bell rang again. When the bell rang again, she stood up and sat down. The gentleman beside her asked, "Why did you do that?" She said, "Everybody else was doing it. I thought I was supposed to." The next time the bell rang, what do you think he did? You probably guessed it; he stood up and sat down with her.

Slowly but surely, what was a random rule for one woman was now the social rule for everybody in the waiting room. We call this kind of internalized behavior social learning. We see what other people do and think, "That's what I want to do because everybody else is doing it." We reward ourselves because we don't want to be excluded. It makes us feel comfortable to conform, but conformity can also lead to bad habits, stunted growth, and status-quo thinking, all of which can plague organizations and cause their downfall.

When we do things just because they have always been done a certain way, we don't progress or look for new solutions. I want to go beyond that. I want to know why we are doing things, why it is essential, and what we are trying to accomplish. I've talked to companies about that because they need to look at how and where they are modeling and fostering curiosity and what action plans they have to avoid status-quo thinking. To create a culture of curiosity, an organization needs to foster the desire to explore and discover.

One of my favorite ways of demonstrating the sense of wonder we had in childhood is by sharing a picture from the San Francisco Museum of Art from *LIFE* magazine published in 1963. The picture shows two adorable little girls who are looking through an air conditioning vent on the wall of the museum to see what's behind it. They are supposed to be looking at all the artwork on the walls—but what do the kids do? They want to see what's behind the vent! We were all that way once, young and asking our parents 100 questions a day. At that age, we're all incredibly curious and want to find out how everything works.

Unfortunately, we eventually lose much of that desire to explore. Research shows that our curiosity peaks around age five and then diminishes sharply. By the time we're in our 30s, it's extremely low. Think about it; when did you stop wanting to look behind the vent? Did somebody say, "Stop that, get up, you're getting dirty?"

We know our level of curiosity diminishes, but how do different groups compare? Are we more or less curious than other people? Merck produced a State of Curiosity Report in 2018 showing that curiosity was higher in larger companies than in smaller ones. Curiosity levels were 37% for large organizations versus 20% small ones. They also found that millennials were more curious than Gen Zs and Boomers. There were also differences by country; the U.S. had more curiosity than China but less than Germany.

Research on curiosity demonstrates the connection between curiosity and the bottom-line benefits organizations hope to improve. When training HR professionals and consultants, I share with them statistics like the ones in Merck's report. However, when training groups of employees, I find that stories like the one about the bell ringing and pictures like the one of the little girls in *LIFE* magazine are more appropriate. Sharing the appropriate illustration or data can demonstrate how important it is to improve our curiosity levels.

CHAPTER 50

Fear

Curiosity will conquer fear even more than bravery will.

—James Stephens

Fear is the first of the four factors in the CCI report. People can fear many things, including failure, embarrassment, or a loss of control. Regarding the fear of embarrassment, nobody wants to say something stupid in a meeting. Instead, we all want to appear smart and well-prepared. We have all been in a meeting when we have no idea what someone is talking about. Not wanting to admit aloud that we're lost, we turn to the person next to us (who often looks lost as well) and ask: "Joe, why don't you ask what he means?" Better that Joe look dumb than us look dumb, right? Naturally, fear of embarrassment is a massive problem in companies. We can also fear appearing confrontational, and as a result organizations can spawn scores of yes-men and yes-women because nobody wants to shake things up or look like they are trying to confront their leaders.

Leaders need to display curiosity so that those they lead can do the same. I want to go back to my old boss who said, "I'm going to pretend I didn't hear that," when I admitted ignorance of something. What he said made me—and would make anyone—feel like an idiot. His response implied that because I didn't know, I should have kept my mouth shut—better to lie and keep up appearances and pretend you know something even if you don't.

Too many leaders say, "Don't come to me with problems unless you have solutions." That might sound good initially because it seems to encourage initiative and discourage whiners and complainers. However, some people can recognize problems even though they don't know how to solve them. If we say to those we lead, "Don't come to me with problems unless you have solutions," that tells them that we actually don't want to know about possible problems the company is having.

In addition to not wanting to look foolish, individuals might also worry that their interests do not align with others'. Many people fear failure. However, having a family or work environment where most see failure as a learning opportunity can allow us to explore ideas we might not have considered. And sometimes we repeat actions or processes because doing so feels familiar. We also avoid certain things in order to feel safe, but doing so can limit us. For example, those who follow a daily routine to feel safe often find that they become bored when things become too routine.

It's easier to overcome fear when we cultivate a positive mindset and enjoy solving complex problems. Additionally, embracing uncertainty allows us to alleviate the discomfort and anxiety often associated with exploration.

A competitive mindset can sometimes generate fear, especially when a person feels that they must always be the smartest person in the room. However, we must not let this mindset hinder us from continuous learning. Desiring knowledge doesn't necessitate intense competition, and interacting with intellectually adept individuals can be both enjoyable and motivating, propelling us to new heights. Always acquaint yourself with everyone you engage with and look for what they can teach you.

While being in the company of knowledgeable individuals might intimidate us, most people willingly share their expertise. Asking questions shows real interest in others and engenders empathy. Through these interactions we conquer intimidation and foster a collaborative environment where everyone shares and appreciates knowledge.

Our past often makes us afraid to break free from status-quo thinking. During our formative years, negative experiences or past failures could have soured us on various subjects. But that which is negative can also be unlearned, and each learning experience is another chance to reshape what was once negative, if done with the right teacher, in the right environment, with the right technology, etc.

Travel, for instance, can broaden our perspectives and ignite our curiosity about subjects like history or geography. Sometimes, revisiting a topic we once disliked might unveil renewed interests, perhaps enabled by delving into a book on that previously avoided subject. Experiences naturally evolve and can give us fresh perspectives that allow us to rediscover our curiosity.

The pressure to succeed can stoke our fears, making us feel overwhelmed and needing more time to fulfill our desires. When priorities weigh heavily, people often spend their downtime on activities that interest them. However, work or family demands can sometimes lead us to relinquish some of our preferred activities, even though they bring us joy.

Life's pressures, especially the pursuit of success, can be daunting. Nevertheless, we must make time for activities that round us out and contribute to our well-being. Many discover that dedicating more time to seemingly trivial pursuits can reveal hidden treasures and open doors to adventure and success, and that exploring uncharted territories can yield unexpected discoveries and enriching experiences.

The fear of having our ideas rejected may lead us to refrain from suggesting anything at all. Because when others disagree with our ideas, we can feel unvalidated or unimportant. While not every idea we come up with will break new ground, unshared ideas won't lead to anything. When we discuss our ideas, even the unpopular ones, we can sometimes spawn new ideas or offshoots from our original idea. Embracing the diverse perspectives that result can further enrich the creative process and foster even more innovative solutions.

Fear of sharing one's ideas stems from the same root cause as the fear of asking questions: being afraid to appear unprepared or incompetent. I have seen many millennials and those who are younger shy away from leadership positions, preferring instead to act as mentors so they can still help but don't have to direct others. Younger generations recognize that each individual brings value to the collective puzzle. No one has all the answers, and sometimes one person alone can make a difference. You don't need to wait until you know everything in order to serve and help. As my friend and world-class speaker Ford Saeks says, "Done is better than perfect," especially when timely delivery matters.

While it may be enticing to project that we have all the answers, many leaders fear having their ignorance discovered. However, effective leaders acknowledge their limits and surround themselves with complementary expertise. Leaders must be willing to share their knowledge while being astute enough to recognize where they themselves lack knowledge. Effective leadership is collaborative and values the knowledge and skills of each team member.

Occasionally, individuals may fear change, especially new roles and new requirements. Adapting to change is never easy, especially when you have to leave behind old ways of doing things to embrace new ways. Sometimes, new leadership requires changes to established practices, so we should keep an open mind and welcome new ideas, especially when those ideas can help everyone progress. This openness can encourage us to explore various ways to succeed as it also sparks creativity. Combining the traditional with the innovative can also yield new ways to accomplish necessary tasks.

Many people naturally seem to resist change. However, in today's dynamic workplace change is a given and must be embraced. Some individuals don't ask questions because they fear their questions will lead to more unforeseen changes. Nevertheless, a world where every day is the same would yield a deadly monotony.

When you suggest an idea that might result in change, it helps to view that idea—and its associated changes—as an opportunity. Embracing change not only helps avoid monotony but also contributes to a more innovative and dynamic workplace. While change is not always easy or comfortable, it can foster creativity and inject new energy into the professional environment.

* * *

To address the challenges identified by this assessment, you must create an effective action plan. For example, if you need to overcome the fear that you must always stay competitive, make sure that when you set goals you make them SMART (specific, measurable, achievable, relevant, and time-bound).

For example, you might avoid researching new subjects because you worry that you might not learn as much as someone else—you fear that sense of competition. When using a SMART goal, begin by choosing a *specific* area to focus on, such as asking questions and showing genuine interest in topics that don't typically appeal to you. Then, to make your goal even more *specific*, ask someone one question a week about a topic they find interesting. To make your goal *measurable,* set an alarm or a note in your calendar to prompt you to ask your question. To make your goal *achievable,* begin with one question per week, which is manageable and allows for gradual progress. To make your goal *relevant,* be sure it aligns with overcoming the fear of competition by fostering genuine interest. To make your goal *time-bound,* commit to asking one question per week over the next month.

To ensure you achieve your goal, actively seek opportunities to engage with different people each week. Demonstrate authentic curiosity and interest in their perspectives and then document the questions and responses to track progress and areas for improvement.

Engage support to reach your goal by informing friends, peers, and family about it. Have them encourage you and remind you to ask questions. And then hold yourself accountable—by using a system—to reinforce this new habit.

Be open to adjusting the goal as needed, based on circumstances or feedback. View any setbacks as opportunities for learning and improvement, and then reassess and modify your action plan as needed.

By following a SMART goal-setting approach and incorporating support mechanisms, you can effectively tackle challenges, build a broader knowledge base, and enhance emotional intelligence through consistent efforts. Remember, the key is to stay committed and to be willing to adapt the plan as you progress.

* * *

Strategies leaders can use to conquer fear and nurture a culture of curiosity require that they understand human psychology, leadership dynamics, and the organizational ecosystem. Consider incorporating the following strategies to dismantle fear and help curiosity to flourish.

Leaders must first foster psychological safety, which is the bedrock of a curious culture and helps individuals feel confident to voice ideas, question assumptions, and engage in open dialogue, all without fear of retribution. Leaders must foster an environment where errors are viewed as valuable learning opportunities rather than punitive setbacks. They can foster this environment by encouraging transparency, actively soliciting input, and demonstrating empathy.

Next, they must conquer fear by cultivating a growth mindset in their employees or those they manage. This mindset believes that one can use dedicated effort to develop their abilities. Organizations that want to foster curiosity need to weave growth mindset principles into their culture. Leaders can use workshops, seminars, and continuous learning programs to empower individuals to embrace challenges, view setbacks as stepping stones to growth, and cultivate resilience.

To conquer fear and improve often requires addressing personal failures. Fear often wears a mask and takes on unique forms based on individual experiences, roles, and perceptions. To conquer fear, it helps to use a system, one where individuals take a journey of self-discovery and reflection. Personalized leadership and development programs can help identify and address fears by offering strategies tailored to overcoming specific hurdles. In doing so, organizations can create a collective narrative of courage and empowerment.

Leaders must let their charges know that every voice matters, so all can feel included. Inclusive decision-making is key to overcoming the fear of judgment. Leaders must actively champion diversity and consider more than one perspective when they make decisions. This strategy extends beyond rhetoric and requires practical methods, such as task forces, cross-functional collaboration, and employee forums, to ensure that every voice is heard and valued.

Leaders must encourage risk-taking and experimentation. The fear of the unknown often stifles curiosity. Thus, organizations must actively encourage calculated risk-taking and experimentation, instilling a culture where innovative ideas are met with enthusiasm rather than skepticism. Establishing innovation labs, project incubators, or designated spaces where employees can experiment can help them explore new ideas on their own. Celebrating both successes and failures builds a resilient mindset that views experimentation as key to learning.

Everyone must commit to using proven strategies to conquer fear. Organizations can build a culture of curiosity when they establish psychological safety, cultivate a growth mindset, address fears, promote inclusive decision-making, and encourage risk-taking. And when they do this, organizations naturally encourage innovation and foster a dynamic and collaborative workplace.

CHAPTER 51

Assumptions

Don't let the noise of others' opinions drown out your own inner voice.

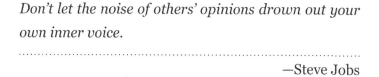

—Steve Jobs

Sometimes our inner voice is positive, but sometimes it talks us out of trying new things. The trick is to know when to listen to it. We make assumptions each time the voice in our head says that something is not interesting or necessary. For instance, our inner voice might say, "I would never be able to do that," or "The last time I did that, they gave me more work."

When I address large audiences, I often make a profound analogy using a bottle of water. I pose the question, "How heavy is this?" Amidst responses like "6 or 8 ounces," I share a transformative insight: the weight doesn't matter; it's how long you have to hold it. It's easy to hold it for a minute. But turn that minute into an hour, or more, and my arm begins to tire. If I hold if for a full day, my arm feels paralyzed. This mirrors our assumptions; fleeting thoughts may *seem* harmless, but over time they can do harm. Thoughts that start as a passing notion can eventually hinder us from pursuing our interests and finding growth. Just like holding that small bottle of water, these thoughts can eventually limit us. The remedy is to recognize this tendency and choose to put the water bottle down (metaphorically speaking) and free ourselves from self-imposed limits.

Assumptions include how we view the world. Some of us feel confident in making crucial decisions because we assume we know the outcome. However, assumptions can also talk us out of exploring new ideas or avenues. The saying "Ignorance is bliss" came about because people often think that more knowledge opens the door to more issues. (Some of these same people also say that "Curiosity killed the cat," so perhaps we shouldn't listen to them at all.)

Having a good level of EQ and IQ can enhance our lives. While some people feel that they have no control over their lives, others thrive by forging their own path. Look for the surprises and wonders in life so you can open up a world of opportunities. Critical thinking skills allow us to analyze life's options, and when we listen with empathy to opposing viewpoints, we can learn to embrace change. Some believe that trying new things wastes time; if so, they might want to question how they spend their time and if it fulfills them. By imagining "what if" scenarios and considering "why not," we open the door to wonder.

Our assumptions come from many sources. Sometimes they arise from snap judgments, where we judge something negatively because it is unfamiliar and no one in our circle has tried it. Lacking any real knowledge, our mind fills in the blanks with a belief that the new encounter will be negative. Our assumptions can also be shaped by our upbringing, and we may need to question why we hold them. One strategy to counter this is to consider the worst-case scenario if we were to try something new, and then determine if liking or disliking it will result in a negative outcome. As we adjust our perspective and challenge our assumptions, we open doors to diverse and enriching experiences.

Sometimes, we deem certain activities as boring due to past experience. For instance, a game might have been tedious when played previously, but when played again with a different person or under different circumstances, it might become much more entertaining. Interestingly, as we age, activities we once thought boring can become exciting. The key lies in giving previously mundane experiences another chance to reveal their potential.

Often, we assume that something new is boring merely because it's unfamiliar. As a result, we stick to activities that align with our past preferences. Whether we binge-watch something because it reminds us of a favorite show or keep reading the same genre of books, we often seek more of what we already enjoy. However, this can hinder us from exploring new and potentially enriching experiences. Instead, we might try taking time each week to read an article about a new topic to break our routine. This intentional diversification can broaden our perspectives and introduce us to unexpected sources of enjoyment.

At times, we don't read or learn about something because we figure it will require too much time or effort. This assumption may come from our belief that we must read an entire book or an entire newspaper to gain knowledge. We put pressure on ourselves to find new knowledge and this can overshadow the joy of exploring new subjects. Just as authors don't write a book in a single sitting, we should not try to consume our knowledge all at once but rather in small increments to make the process more manageable. When we take small steps to work on long-term learning objectives, we allow ourselves to acquire new knowledge without feeling overwhelmed.

We often convince ourselves that ignorance is bliss and that no news is good news, as the saying goes. Some even assume that if they remain uninformed about an issue, then that issue ceases to exist. However, there is a universe of information out there waiting for us to uncover it. By itself, knowledge is valuable and good; it's how people act on that knowledge that can cause problems. For instance, learning about poverty might initially feel uncomfortable, but that learning is necessary to try to find solutions. When we avoid problems, they don't disappear; instead, we must confront them and understand them to make any real progress.

Sometimes, individuals don't share their ideas because they fear they'll be asked to head a committee or be given additional responsibilities. And for good reason; employees often generate innovative ideas, only to find themselves rewarded with increased workloads. No wonder some try to avoid this discouraging outcome. Effective communication between employees and employers can help overcome this hurdle. Employers need to make clear what happens when employees present a good idea. If they reward, rather than burden, their employees, those employees are more likely to share their ideas. If employers expect more work from employees who propose a good idea, then employees should seek appropriate compensation, which makes negotiation an essential tactic they need to use.

Often, we talk ourselves out of pursuing extra activities because we've witnessed others do the same but get no apparent rewards. Even if new information does not seem life-changing, it can later create future learning opportunities. The value of acquiring knowledge may only become evident when we apply it in practical scenarios, such as using algebra to calculate a restaurant tip or to figure out which trip route will use less gas. We might think that learning something new is futile when people struggle but still fail to achieve expected results. However, even negative outcomes can teach us what doesn't work—and why.

Occasionally, we avoid doing something because we believe that the end result won't meet our needs or expectations. Other times, we feel discouraged by a perceived lack of progress even though we've worked hard. In such situations, we should seek guidance to overcome these barriers to achieving our goals. We should also surround ourselves with mentors and individuals with more knowledge than we have. When we are in the dark, it helps to be near those who can shine the light of experience and help us surmount our current obstacles.

At times, we talk ourselves out of new endeavors because we dismiss them as not being worth the effort. As a result, some restrict their interests to a narrow scope because they fail to see personal benefits. In such cases, life coaches can help us transform our lives and achieve our goals. Those who have yet to feel the joy of accomplishing something new are missing out on one of life's sublime experiences. When we can hear others' stories about their achievements and the emotions they felt, the mental picture we form can help us stay focused on our ultimate goal.

* * *

Identify a Challenge: Our tendency to avoid new experiences or topics based on assumptions developed from past encounters.

Set a SMART Goal: Begin by selecting a specific activity, such as engaging in new conversations or trying activities you assume are uninteresting. To make it *specific*, commit to asking one question per week about a new topic (one you assume is uninteresting). To make it *measurable*, set a weekly reminder (on your calendar or an alarm) to initiate this interaction. To make it *achievable*, start with one question per week to allow gradual progress. To make it *relevant*, ensure the goal directly addresses the challenge of assuming disinterest and promotes genuine exploration. To make it *time-bound*, commit to asking one question per week over the next month.

Execution and Implementation: Actively seek opportunities to engage in conversations or activities related to topics you assume are uninteresting. Record your experiences and observations to track progress and reflect on your changing perceptions.

Engage Support: Share your goal with friends, peers, or family, to get their encouragement and suggestions for new activities or topics. Establish a support system to reinforce commitment and provide positive encouragement.

Flexibility and Adaptation: Stay open to adjusting the goal based on feedback or evolving circumstances. Embrace setbacks as learning opportunities, and regularly assess and modify your action plan to accommodate changing preferences or interests. Through this SMART goal and support system, overcome the challenge of assuming disinterest and cultivate a mindset that embraces new experiences with genuine curiosity.

* * *

Cognitive diversity counters assumption-making and challenges conventional thinking as it promotes new perspectives. Organizations must actively embrace diversity in experiences, backgrounds, and cognitive styles to break free from the shackles of assumption. Initiatives such as mentorship programs, cross-functional teams, and diversity-focused hiring practices can help build a workplace where varied viewpoints dismantle assumptions, paving the way for unbiased curiosity.

Assumptions often lurk in the shadows of our unconscious biases and shape our perceptions without us being aware of it. Organizations can launch assumption awareness programs that shed light on these blind spots, fostering self-reflection and a heightened awareness of our biases. Through workshops, training sessions, and continuous education, individuals can develop the skills to recognize and challenge assumptions, enabling them to embrace curiosity more readily and directly.

Silos within organizational structures can breed assumptions, limiting information flow and hindering collaboration. To overcome this, organizations should encourage their workers to work together and share knowledge across departments. The resulting cross-functional teams, interdepartmental projects, and collaborative platforms can help an organization replace its assumptions with shared understanding and foster unbiased curiosity.

Assumptions often arise when individuals don't question the status quo. Organizations must instill a culture of proactive inquiry, where questioning is not only encouraged but celebrated. Leaders must set the tone and emphasize asking thoughtful questions and challenging assumptions. Organizations can use forums, brainstorming, and innovation hubs to help dismantle assumptions and encourage the continuous pursuit of knowledge.

In this information age, leveraging technology can help dispel assumptions. Organizations should harness data analytics and artificial intelligence to gain objective insights and minimize subjective assumptions. When organizations use technology to help them make decisions, they ensure that curiosity is grounded in evidence, and they foster a culture that consistently challenges assumptions and replaces them with data-backed exploration. Dispelling assumptions requires that organizations use a multifaceted approach that includes cognitive diversity, assumption awareness programs, cross-functional collaboration, proactive inquiry, and the strategic use of technology. By dismantling the assumption-making process, organizations can help curiosity flourish, unlock innovation and cultivate an atmosphere that values diverse perspectives.

CHAPTER 52

Technology

I fear the day that technology will surpass our human interaction. The world will have a generation of idiots.

—Albert Einstein

Technology, whether over- or under-utilized, has significantly shaped our curiosity. Technology can either facilitate our curiosity when seamlessly performing tasks on our behalf, or it can block our curiosity, especially when we lack adequate training or feel overwhelmed by its complexities. Technology can also shape our childhood experiences and lay the foundation for curiosity, either for good or for ill.

One positive example of technology's effect on curiosity during childhood is Steve Wozniak. In his autobiography, *iWoz*, he wrote about how his dad inspired him to play with gadgets. His father would come home from work carrying wires and components and show Steve how the electronics should be connected, why this wire was necessary, how it brought electricity, and so on. And although Wozniak benefited from that experience, that is not the case for everyone.

Some of us rarely think about how technology works because it does so much for us every day. While technology has opened a world of opportunities, we rely on it and sometimes fear it. Some of us avoid using technology or consider it an impediment to learning. On the other hand, many are so dependent on social media that they base decisions and choices on what their friends might do. Others are so turned off by social media that they avoid it altogether. The Internet offers a world of knowledge, but keeping up with every advance can be challenging. While some people want to keep up with all the latest gadgets, others would rather someone explain how to use them rather than explore how they work. Some careers require that you have skills. And yet many workers hold onto old ways of doing things because these worked well in the past. Embracing technological change often requires proactive preparation. What communication advantages would we miss if we still had only landlines (you know, the phones attached to the wall)? While some think of technology only as playing around on computers, others view it as an effective tool. Technology takes time to learn to use, but in the end it can save time.

Some individuals have convinced themselves that certain technologies are not worth learning. It's easy to see why. While computers can automate various tasks, their efficacy is not always guaranteed. On the other hand, some of the most successful entrepreneurs owe their achievements to understanding and using technology, especially in business. Before you can create the next groundbreaking invention that enhances the quality of life, you must first grasp technology's fundamentals.

Some individuals avoid acquiring new knowledge because they feel they lack the right information to delve deeper. Others may find technology intriguing but hesitate to start from the beginning, fearing the work involved in catch up with others. It's important to recognize that the rapid pace of change means everyone is, in some sense, starting anew when they learn about technology. Even though we may feel far behind, this may not actually be the case. To learn about technology, it helps to spend time one-on-one with someone who possesses a solid foundation and has hands-on experience with technology, who can teach you more than any book could. Technology enthusiasts are often willing to share their knowledge, so don't hesitate to reach out to them and ask for guidance.

At times, we may be unaware of technology's benefits if we've had limited exposure to it. To broaden our understanding, dive into some of the copious literature that covers new and emerging technologies and seek guidance from individuals who have substantial experience in technology. Reflect on what you envision technology can do for you, and run your ideas by a few experts. Even if the technology you seek does not currently exist, proposing innovative suggestions can pave the way for future advancements.

Some older adults are hesitant to learn new technology because it was not part of their upbringing. Others may come from environments or periods where technology was not widely embraced, causing them to be uncomfortable with the unfamiliar. We must not automatically assume that technology is challenging or negative just because we haven't been exposed to it.

Often the best remedy is to take small steps to learn the basics so we can gradually embrace newer technologies.

Technology's ever-changing nature can also frustrate many individuals. It seems that just as we become adept at using a particular program or device, a new one takes its place. It's akin to walking on a treadmill and being constantly in motion. However, just like walking on a treadmill, if we stop, we risk falling off and making no progress, so we must continue to move forward and learn. Embracing the continuous discovery of what lies ahead is part of the joy of technology. Like opening presents on a holiday morning, grappling with the unknown workings of a new device is both challenging and ultimately rewarding.

Occasionally, individuals convince themselves that they lack the time or education to fully comprehend technology. Falling behind on learning the latest versions can contribute to this mindset. If you find yourself using an older version of a particular technology, you need to question what might be holding you back. If time is a concern, consider how much time you'll need to spend to learn when the technology changes again. Technological advancements often bring new and intriguing features, and there's an opportunity cost associated with not investing time in staying updated. While the time you need to spend learning a new technology may seem significant, the benefits it can provide usually often outweigh these concerns.

Individuals often aren't sure where to start when learning technology. For starters, not everyone needs to be a technological genius, and one can resolve many computer-related issues easily with a basic understanding of how things work. Knowing simple tasks, like how to format a document, can significantly enhance one's productivity. Fortunately, social media platforms offer a plethora of instructional videos covering a wide range of technological topics. Watching these videos leads to a sense of accomplishment for those who learn to address minor issues that were previously slowing them down.

Critical thinking skills can also help one learn to master arcane technology. While technology may initially seem baffling, it can become less so when we take the time to understand how computers, phones, and other devices operate. When we cultivate our sense of wonder and curiosity, we open our minds to the ways these devices can assist us. We need to recognize that practical minds, as well as those with high-tech expertise, can create innovative solutions. When we encourage others to understand technology, we motivate them to problem-solve and innovate.

Technology has generated an unprecedented abundance of data, which can be challenging to manage. It's unrealistic to expect us to comprehend the intricacies of everything or consume vast amounts of content in a short order. Even though we all have 24 hours in a day, what may be manageable for one person can easily overwhelm another. Therefore, learning capacities are not comparable, and we should set realistic expectations based on our personal capabilities and do our best but do it at our own pace.

* * *

Identify a Challenge: Consider the reluctance to explore and learn how to use new technologies, particularly technology like ChatGPT or some other AI-driven software, while maintaining a status-quo mindset that deems such knowledge unnecessary.

Set a SMART Goal: Start by focusing on a *specific* aspect, such as embracing curiosity about using ChatGPT. To make it *specific*, commit to learning one new feature of ChatGPT per week. To make it *measurable*, set weekly reminders on your calendar to learn a feature. To make it *achievable*, start with one inquiry per week about ChatGPT, allowing for gradual progress. To make it *relevant*, ensure your goal aligns with overcoming the status-quo mindset and fosters genuine curiosity about using new technology like ChatGPT. To make it *time-bound*, dedicate time each week to learning one aspect of using ChatGPT over the next month.

Execution and Implementation: Actively seek opportunities to explore and learn how to use ChatGPT for various tasks. Record your discoveries and observations to track your progress and reflect on your changing perceptions.

Engage Support: Share your goal with friends, peers, or family and seek their encouragement and suggestions for using ChatGPT. Establish a support system to reinforce your commitment and provide positive reinforcement.

Flexibility and Adaptation: Stay open to adjusting the goal based on feedback or evolving circumstances. Embrace setbacks as learning opportunities and regularly assess and modify your action plan to accommodate changing preferences or interests. Through this SMART goal and support system, you can overcome your reluctance to learn a new technology, such as ChatGPT, and embrace curiosity and technical proficiency.

* * *

To harness curiosity effectively, organizations should design learning initiatives. Curiosity thrives where people are continually learning and where they view challenges as opportunities. When organizations implement training programs, workshops, and skill-building sessions, they encourage their employees to explore new ideas and acquire diverse skills, ultimately fueling organizational growth.

Organizations can create physical or virtual spaces dedicated to curiosity. Known as curiosity hubs, these spaces serve as focal points for exploration and idea generation. These hubs give employees a dedicated space in which to brainstorm, experiment, and collaborate on innovative projects. By actively fostering curiosity, organizations tap into their workforce's creative potential, leading to groundbreaking solutions and advancements.

Organizations must acknowledge and reward curious behavior to reinforce its value. When organizations establish recognition programs and employee incentives to reward them for demonstrating curiosity, they let their employees know that they are committed to fostering exploration. This recognition, which can include awards, promotions, or special projects, creates a positive feedback loop that sustains curiosity.

Curiosity flourishes when individuals can connect with diverse perspectives. Organizations can create cross-functional networks that bring together employees from different departments and disciplines. These networks provide a platform for knowledge sharing, collaborative problem-solving, and ideas cross-pollination. By fostering connections among curious minds, organizations are better able to tackle complex challenges and drive innovation.

To keep curiosity a strategic imperative, organizations should integrate it into their performance metrics and key performance indicators (KPIs). By aligning individual and team goals with curiosity-driven outcomes, organizations are signaling to their employees that exploration and innovation are important. Performance evaluations can assess how employees contribute to a culture of curiosity, thus reinforcing its significance.

To nurture curiosity, organizations should design learning initiatives, establish dedicated exploration spaces, recognize and reward curious behavior, build cross-functional networks, and integrate curiosity into performance metrics. By strategically utilizing curiosity, organizations unlock their workforce's full potential, which in turn drives innovation and maintains future growth.

CHAPTER 53

Environment

Being nosey weakens a relationship, being curious strengthens it.

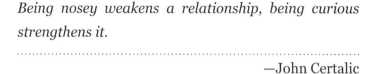

—John Certalic

Our environment impacts us profoundly and includes influences from teachers, family, friends, social media, leaders, peers, past leaders, and everyone we've ever collaborated with professionally. The collective presence of individuals who have traversed our lives has shaped how we developed, or failed to develop, our curiosity.

As I mentioned in a previous chapter, our curiosity peaks around age five and then declines, and one cause for that decline is our educational system. Standardized testing and its demands often leave teachers with little time to cultivate curiosity as they navigate students' demands while attempting to prepare them to meet prescribed educational benchmarks. When these teachers feel compelled to "teach to the test," they often have little or no time to delve into questions that don't align with the test content, which leaves little time for exploration.

In the past, our school options were often more limited compared to the diverse offerings available today. Schools typically had a set curriculum with a fixed number of courses, and some might have only offered one language. Educators too might have been influenced by old adages such as "kids should be seen and not heard," which reflected a more restrictive mindset. This could inadvertently discourage the exploration of topics that captured our childhood curiosity. Fortunately, some of us had teachers who allowed us to explore, although such teachers might not have been the norm.

Family, teachers, friends, and social media can also affect our curiosity, both through their expectations and when they inadvertently discourage us from going where we want. As we grew up, we may have heard sayings like "Curiosity killed the cat," which some used to keep us from getting into too much trouble but which also discouraged exploration. Those of us who naturally think outside the box were probably not rewarded for it or were told not to be complicated.

Siblings and peers in particular can also negatively influence a child's curiosity, especially when they deliver sometimes harsh critiques whenever the child deviates from others' perceived notions of what is "cool." At times people follow their peers, regardless of the consequences. And so, while our friends sometimes like things that we might not, we might go along to get along and end up doing activities that did not inspire our curiosity.

Our work life can also negatively influence our curiosity. At times, our professional roles can become narrowly focused due to our expertise in a specific area. Work leaders too may exhibit a limited focus, seeking information only within their narrow scope. This approach can discourage a broader perspective, which in turn discourages curiosity. In another vein, some companies solicit suggestions but may not implement these ideas, despite their merit, due to resource constraints or other factors.

As a result of pressure at work not to be curious or rock the company boat, individuals may hesitate to provide suggestions for fear of reprisal. They may also fail to make suggestions if they fear they may have to assume additional responsibilities, even if these are compensated. Maintaining a minimal workload, comfortable as it might be, can become monotonous without room for personal or professional growth. It's crucial to recognize that ideas requiring more effort can lead to expanded opportunities for advancement and financial rewards, encouraging a more fulfilling and rewarding professional journey.

As cultural norms evolve, so does our perspective on curiosity. Thus, while we cannot alter the past, acknowledging its impact on our curiosity and inclination to ask questions is a crucial step forward.

With that in mind, you may want to consider revisiting jobs or subjects that once intrigued you in your youth. Researching those areas may reignite a spark and allow you to delve deeper into subjects of personal interest. You may also wish to reflect on the limitations of the schools you attended. If the language taught didn't capture your interest, there may have been other languages you could have found interesting. Your exposure to different cultures through travel could have sparked newfound interests that weren't explored in the past.

Given that families influence our curiosity, it might help to reflect on personal aspirations you may have overlooked due to familial expectations and explore new possibilities that align with individual interests and goals.

The same goes for friend and peer relationships, where our desire to fit in or avoid conflict may have led to us not doing what interested us and pursuing interests that weren't ours. Conflict is a natural aspect of all close relationships. Constantly prioritizing others' preferences over our own can lead to feelings of resentment. Effectively addressing this involves open and respectful communication, expressing our likes and dislikes, and working toward mutual agreements that consider everyone's needs. It also might help to connect with like-minded individuals who share similar interests while also being mindful not to unintentionally dismiss others' ideas and to encourage an open-minded approach that goes beyond groupthink.

We can also make changes in our professional life. If we've learned leadership from individuals whose view was very narrow, it's essential to consider the missed opportunities that could arise from a more open-minded approach. To improve your curiosity, you might try adopting a broader view in professional settings.

Some may have faced negative experiences in the past when they tried to make suggestions at work. Going forward, it might help to inquire as to why they weren't implemented. Asking questions about how to enhance the value of these ideas and seeking feedback can serve as a reminder to those who may have overlooked them initially.

* * *

Identify a Challenge: Reflect on childhood experiences where teachers did not answer all your questions, which inhibited your curiosity. Now there is a need to rediscover the things that used to interest you as a kid.

Set a SMART Goal: Begin by focusing on reigniting curiosity about topics that captivated you as a child. To make it *specific*, commit to exploring one topic or activity each week that used to capture your interest. To make it *measurable*, set reminders on your calendar or alarms to dedicate time weekly to rediscovering these childhood interests. To make it *achievable*, make one inquiry per week into a topic or activity that intrigued you as a child. To make it *relevant*, ensure that the goal helps you overcome unanswered questions from childhood. To make it *time-bound*, dedicate time each week to rediscovering one aspect of your childhood interests over the next month.

Execution and Implementation: Actively seek opportunities to revisit and explore topics or activities that captivated you as a child. Record your discoveries and observations to track progress and reconnect with those interests.

Engage Support: Share your goal with friends, peers, or family, and seek their encouragement and suggestions to rediscover childhood interests. Establish a support system to bolster your commitment and provide positive reinforcement.

Flexibility and Adaptation: Stay open to adjusting the goal based on feedback or evolving circumstances. Embrace setbacks as learning opportunities and regularly assess and modify the action plan to accommodate changing preferences or interests. Through this SMART goal and support system, you can overcome the challenge of unanswered questions that inhibited childhood curiosity so you can rediscover and embrace your early interests.

* * *

A sustained, curiosity-centric culture begins with strong leadership commitment. Leaders must actively demonstrate and advocate for curiosity as a core value. By setting the tone, leaders inspire employees at all levels to embrace curiosity as part of their work. Leaders need to make this commitment evident in both words and actions, reinforcing the organization's dedication to fostering a dynamic and innovative environment.

Organizations must embrace continuous learning and adaptation. This involves cultivating a culture where change is viewed not as a disruption but as a growth opportunity. Curiosity becomes a driving force in navigating uncertainties as leaders encourage employees to seek new knowledge, adapt to evolving circumstances, and actively help the organization to thrive.

Establishing feedback loops is crucial for learning from curiosity-driven initiatives. Organizations should gather insights, lessons learned, and success stories that arise from curiosity-centric projects. They can use regular feedback sessions, retrospectives, and knowledge-sharing forums that provide valuable information to refine strategies, identify best practices, and enhance the organization's nurturing of curiosity.

A sustainable curiosity-centric culture thrives on inclusion and diversity. Organizations should actively promote diverse perspectives, backgrounds, and experiences within their workforce.

Inclusive environments encourage individuals to bring their unique insights to the table, fostering a rich collection of ideas. By embracing diversity, organizations create a robust foundation for curiosity to flourish and drive innovative solutions to complex challenges.

To sustain a curiosity-centric culture, organizations should integrate curiosity into their core values. This involves incorporating curiosity as a guiding principle that aligns with the organization's mission and vision. When curiosity becomes inseparable from an organization's identity, it permeates all aspects of work, decision-making, and interactions. This integration ensures that curiosity continues to shape the organization's trajectory.

Leaders must commit to sustaining a curiosity-centric culture. They must also provide continuous learning and adaptation, establish feedback loops, focus on inclusion and diversity, and integrate curiosity into core values. By doing all this, leaders and their organizations can permanently embed curiosity into their culture, driving ongoing success and adaptability in an ever-changing landscape.

PART X

TAKING ACTION

While this book is designed for everyone who wants to learn how curiosity can positively impact business and help you (and your business) escape status-quo thinking, the following chapters—leading up to the Conclusion—will interest leaders, consultants, and HR professionals the most. If you find this content less than relevant to your current role or aren't yet ready to dive into the level of detail included here, feel free to jump to the Conclusion—literally!

Fostering a curiosity-based culture is not just an aspiration but a strategic imperative. The lessons learned from successful individuals, organizational failures, and the transformative power of curiosity paint a detailed roadmap for organizations seeking to harness unlimited potential and possibilities.

Leadership plays a pivotal role in setting the tone for organizational culture. Leaders must actively embody and promote curiosity. This involves asking questions, encouraging exploration, and showcasing the value of continuous learning. When leaders embrace curiosity, that mindset permeates the organization.

Organizations should create structures that incentivize curiosity. Recognizing and rewarding employees for asking questions, proposing innovative solutions, and engaging in continuous learning fosters a culture where curiosity is encouraged and celebrated.

Organizations must allocate resources to research and development initiatives. They should also invest in projects that encourage exploration, experimentation, and the pursuit of new ideas—and this proactive approach to research positions the organization at the forefront of innovation.

A diverse and inclusive workplace fosters curiosity by bringing in individuals with varied perspectives and experiences. Encouraging collaboration among various teams cultivates an environment where different viewpoints contribute to creative problem-solving and innovation.

Implementing training and development programs that explicitly focus on cultivating curiosity is essential. These programs can include workshops, seminars, and mentorship opportunities that instill a mindset of continuous learning and exploration.

And embracing a mindset of continuous learning is fundamental. Individuals actively seeking knowledge, questioning assumptions, and exploring new horizons are better positioned to unlock their unlimited potential. This involves a commitment to personal and professional development throughout one's career.

Curiosity inherently promotes adaptability. Individuals who cultivate a curious mindset are more agile in navigating change and embracing new opportunities. Adaptability opens the door to unlimited possibilities in both the personal and professional spheres.

Curiosity is a catalyst for innovative problem-solving. By questioning the status quo and exploring unconventional solutions, individuals can tackle challenges creatively and ingeniously, unlocking new pathways to success.

Building connections with diverse individuals and fostering collaborative relationships broadens one's horizons. Networking and collaborating with others provides access to new ideas, perspectives, and potential opportunities yet to be discovered.

Curiosity emboldens individuals to take calculated risks and bounce back from setbacks. Viewing challenges as learning opportunities and being resilient in the face of failure allows individuals to push boundaries and explore uncharted territories.

The insights gained from this book's exploration underscore the transformative power of curiosity in shaping successful individuals and organizations. Moving forward, the emphasis should be on a collective effort to embed curiosity into the DNA of organizations and individuals.

This involves a commitment to ongoing research, a cultural shift prioritizing curiosity, and proactive steps to incentivize and celebrate curiosity-driven initiatives. By embracing a curiosity-based culture, organizations can not only navigate the complexities of a rapidly changing world but also unlock unlimited potential and possibilities.

As we propel ourselves into the future, the rallying cry is clear: curiosity is not just a trait but a force that drives us toward new frontiers, fuels innovation and ensures that our collective journey is marked by continuous exploration and growth. The possibilities are boundless, and the key to unlocking them lies in cultivating a culture where curiosity is encouraged and revered as the driving force behind transformative success.

CHAPTER 54

Metrics

Live a life full of humility, gratitude, intellectual curiosity, and never stop learning. Curiosity is the lust of the mind. Once we believe in ourselves, we can risk curiosity, wonder, spontaneous delight, or any experience that reveals the human spirit.

—Gza

By now, you have learned how critical curiosity is to the success of your organization. But how do you implement a culture of curiosity?

The first step is to realize that implementing such a culture is nothing less than critical to achieving innovation, engagement, and a workplace culture that rewards everyone. For individuals to improve, they must first recognize what inhibits them. Analyzing survey results and identifying patterns, weaknesses, and potential opportunities is a critical part of this process. Leaders must emulate the culture they hope to achieve and use survey findings to identify priorities.

It can be tempting to try to change everything all at once, but that can be overwhelming. Instead, start by identifying several areas that inhibit people. As leaders adopt culture change, they must communicate its benefits and successes to members of the organization. Organizations that create cross-functional teams succeed because they assign a representative to implement cultural changes.

As with any change, you must establish clear goals and a well-communicated strategy. Inform employees about expected outcomes from this process and allow them to identify issues that affect them and the larger organization. Provide employees with a kick-off training program to show them what has inhibited individuals, and follow that up with continued training and development to further hone positive skills and behaviors.

Track and measure incremental changes to ensure continued progress. It also helps to develop KPIs and follow-up surveys. Schedule regular meetings to assess what has worked and what hasn't to ensure that the new culture becomes the norm. Some organizations have successfully hired consultants to ensure these new behaviors stick or to address any challenging issues. As with any change, undertake periodic reviews and make any needed refinements to ensure that the change adheres.

One of the most important things leaders can do is showcase curiosity champions, similar to what Verizon did when they shared my vision and highlighted employees' success stories when they embraced curiosity (see Chapter 11). Such champions can inspire others to become more curious, so it's wise to reward and recognize them. Moreover, celebrating individuals who have achieved positive outcomes demonstrates organizational buy-in to the overall effort. You may also want to change employee workspaces to further encourage cross-functional collaboration.

To make it simpler visually, consider the following steps:

- Begin with assessing levels and surveying employees.
- Next, identify critical areas to improve and how leadership should align themselves.
- Develop a curiosity vision and integrate curiosity into the core values while communicating the proposed strategy.
- Align training and development to help create a curiosity-based environment.
- Choose curiosity champions and incorporate curiosity into performance metrics.
- Establish feedback mechanisms and make this an iterative process, addressing barriers and measuring progress.

Remember that cultural change takes time, and creating a curious culture requires an ongoing effort and commitment from the entire organization.

* * *

As you incorporate curiosity into the culture, you must determine the metrics that will ensure successful change. Leaders should ask what aspects of curiosity align with their objectives and break down specific behaviors or competencies to measure. For example, a company's sales division can benefit when they ask their customers insightful questions and, more importantly, listen to the answers so the division can create sales presentations that address those customers' desired benefits.

Therefore, the organization must learn to ask insightful questions, explore new ideas, seek diverse perspectives, and be willing to learn. What competencies are required for that to occur? Employees need inquisitive thinking, which requires asking thoughtful questions and exploring potential solutions. They also need to demonstrate open-mindedness by being receptive to new ideas and perspectives. They should embrace continuous learning in order to build their knowledge and skills, and they should engage in cross-functional collaboration.

Next, find a way to measure the above. Measuring inquisitive thinking might entail counting how many insightful questions are asked during a sales presentation. For open-mindedness, individuals could demonstrate acceptance of diverse viewpoints during cross-functional meetings. Organizations could easily measure continuous learning by logging completed training courses or certification programs. Measure collaborative exploration by logging employee involvement in interdepartmental projects or initiatives.

To quantify all this, you must first set goals. For inquisitive thinking, perhaps set a goal to ask several meaningful questions per quarter. For open-mindedness, set a goal to spend a percentage of time participating in cross-functional activities, and measure continuous learning by tracking training hours. Measure collaborative exploration by setting a goal to contribute to at least one cross-functional project per year. There are multiple ways to obtain feedback on how things improve, including employee surveys, performance reviews, and 360-degree feedback.

Organizations should include curiosity metrics in performance reviews to ensure they are integrating the change, and the training and development department should encourage the development of inquisitive thinking, open-mindedness, continuous learning, and collaborative exploration.

* * *

You may want to consider using the following steps and potential metrics:

- *Define Curiosity Metrics:* Clearly define how curiosity aligns with the organization's objectives. Consider breaking down curiosity into specific behaviors or competencies you can measure.
- *Training and Development Metrics:* Measure employees' participation in curiosity-related training programs. This could include the number of courses completed, workshops attended, or certifications earned.
- *Innovation and Creativity Metrics:* Tie curiosity to innovation and creativity metrics. Measure the number of innovative ideas generated and implemented projects resulting from curiosity-driven initiatives or patents filed.
- *Cross-functional Collaboration Metrics:* Evaluate employees' ability to collaborate across departments or teams. Metrics could include the frequency of cross-functional projects, successful collaboration outcomes, or improvements in interdepartmental communication.
- *Project Ownership and Initiative Metrics:* Assess employees' willingness to take ownership of projects and initiatives. Measure the number of self-driven projects, successful outcomes, or contributions to developing new initiatives.

- *Problem-Solving Metrics:* Evaluate employees' problem-solving skills, as curiosity often helps with seeking innovative solutions. Metrics could include the successful resolution of complex issues, the introduction of new problem-solving methodologies, or improvements in decision-making.

- *Learning and Adaptability Metrics:* Measure employees' ability to learn and adapt to new situations. This could include the speed at which employees acquire new skills, the successful application of learning in their roles, or adaptability in the face of change.

- *Customer Engagement Metrics:* Connect curiosity to customer engagement and satisfaction. Metrics may include developing customer-centric initiatives, improving customer feedback scores, or successfully implementing customer-driven enhancements.

- *Feedback and Improvement Metrics:* Evaluate employees' openness to feedback and commitment to continuous improvement. Metrics could include the frequency of feedback-seeking behavior, the successful implementation of feedback-driven changes, or improvements in work processes.

- *Knowledge-sharing Metrics:* Measure employees' willingness to share knowledge with colleagues. Metrics could include the frequency of knowledge-sharing initiatives, the development of internal resources, or improvements in team collaboration.

- *Curiosity Assessments:* Utilize a curiosity index to determine the factors that inhibit curiosity. Also, provide an assessment that measures curiosity within the organization.

- *Performance Reviews and Goal-attainment Metrics:* Integrate curiosity-related competencies into performance reviews and goal-setting processes. Assess employees based on their ability to demonstrate curiosity and its positive impact on achieving organizational objectives.

- *Recognition and Rewards Metrics:* Tie curiosity to recognition and rewards programs. Acknowledge and reward employees who consistently exhibit curiosity and contribute to the organization's success.

- *Surveys and Assessments:* Implement periodic surveys or assessments to gather feedback on employees' perceived curiosity levels. Use this data to identify areas for improvement and track changes over time.

* * *

To create a culture of curiosity, consider the following example timeline:

- **STEP 1: Leadership Alignment and Commitment** (Timeline: 3-6 months)
  a. *Assessment and Buy-In:* Conduct an organizational assessment to identify current levels of curiosity and the factors that inhibit it. Engage leaders in discussions about the benefits of curiosity and its impact on innovation and problem-solving.

b. *Curiosity Champions:* Identify and appoint leaders across various departments as "Curiosity Champions." These champions will spearhead initiatives, communicate the vision, and inspire others to embrace curiosity.

c. *Training for Leadership:* Provide leadership training on fostering curiosity. Equip leaders with tools to encourage open dialogue, embrace diverse perspectives, and create a psychologically safe environment.

- **STEP 2: Communication and Awareness**
  (Timeline: Ongoing)

  a. *Launch Campaigns:* Implement ongoing communication campaigns that highlight curiosity's importance. To reinforce the message, utilize multiple channels such as emails, internal newsletters, and posters.

  b. *Storytelling Sessions:* Organize regular storytelling sessions where employees share when curiosity led to positive outcomes. These stories create a narrative around the value of curiosity within the organization.

  c. *Leadership Visibility:* Ensure leaders actively communicate and model curiosity. Encourage leaders to share their learning experiences, demonstrating vulnerability and a commitment to continuous improvement.

- **STEP 3: Training and Development**
  (Timeline: 6-12 months)

  a. *Curiosity Workshops:* Implement workshops that focus on building curiosity skills. These workshops can cover active listening, asking powerful questions, and fostering a growth mindset.

  b. *External Training Programs:* Invest in external programs or bring in experts to conduct specialized training sessions on creativity, innovation, and curiosity. Provide ongoing opportunities for skill development.

  c. *Learning Platforms:* Integrate curiosity-focused content into existing learning platforms. Offer resources like webinars, articles, and interactive modules to facilitate self-directed learning.

- **STEP 4: Recognition and Rewards**
  (Timeline: Ongoing)

  a. *Curiosity Awards:* Establish an award system to recognize individuals or teams demonstrating exceptional curiosity. Celebrate their achievements through company-wide communications and ceremonies.

  b. *Performance Metrics:* Integrate curiosity-related metrics into performance evaluations. During appraisal cycles, recognize and reward employees who actively contribute to a culture of curiosity.

  c. *Peer Recognition:* Implement a peer recognition system where employees can acknowledge and appreciate each other's curiosity-driven contributions. This fosters a collaborative and supportive environment.

- **STEP 5: Integration with Existing Processes**
  (Timeline: 6-12 months)
  a. *Performance Goals:* Align individual and team performance goals with curiosity-related objectives. This ensures that curiosity becomes an integral part of day-to-day work.
  b. *Innovation Frameworks:* Embed curiosity within innovation frameworks. Encourage employees to explore unconventional solutions, and reward experimentation.
  c. *Feedback Mechanisms:* Establish regular feedback loops to measure curiosity initiatives' effectiveness. Continually use this feedback to refine and enhance the program.

- **STEP 6: Measurement and Continuous Improvement** (Timeline: Ongoing)
  a. *Metrics Dashboard:* Develop a metrics dashboard that tracks key indicators of curiosity, such as participation in training programs, the frequency of knowledge-sharing, and the success of curiosity-driven projects.
  b. *Surveys and Feedback:* Conduct regular surveys to gauge employee perceptions of the organization's curiosity culture. Use feedback to identify areas for improvement and tailor initiatives accordingly.
  c. *Continuous Refinement:* Continuously refine your culture of curiosity initiatives based on data and feedback. Flexibility and adaptability are essential to maintaining a dynamic and evolving culture.

By following these detailed steps, organizations can systematically create and nurture a culture of curiosity, fostering innovation, collaboration, and continuous learning.

CHAPTER 55

Training and Workshop

Curiosity is the wick in the candle of learning.

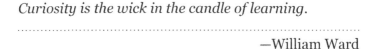

—William Ward

When training consultants and HR professionals to become CCI-certified, I provide them with scripts and training materials. While I don't have room here to duplicate all of these materials, I have included some information to help HR, leaders, and consultants convey a curiosity culture's value to an organization.

Introducing Curiosity to Leaders

Fostering a culture of curiosity requires leaders and employees to make significant changes. And how you introduce curiosity's value depends on whether you present to leaders or employees. Leaders want more quantitative reasoning. They want to know what's in it for them, how it impacts the bottom line, what the change entails, and so on. Initial presentations to them should be short enough to keep their attention but detailed enough to answer these questions.

To introduce the value of creating a culture of curiosity to leaders, consider the following slides:

1. **Welcome & Introduction to Curiosity**

   Begin with a warm welcome and introduce the concept of curiosity. Highlight its critical role in driving innovation, adaptation, and productivity. Emphasize the importance of understanding and overcoming the four inhibitors of curiosity.

2. **The Value of Curiosity**

   Discuss the tangible benefits of fostering curiosity within the organization. Use data and research to underline its impact on engagement, innovation, and competitive advantage. Examples of data:

   - *Key to innovation*: A study published in the *Harvard Business Review* highlights that curiosity is the key to innovation. Fostering curiosity in the workplace can lead to a 34% increase in creativity and innovative thinking among employees. Additionally, a report by Deloitte emphasizes that organizations with adaptable employees are 1.5 times more likely to achieve above-average financial returns, underlining the importance of curiosity-driven adaptability.

   - *Boost innovation and creativity*: A survey conducted by McKinsey found that 84% of executives believe innovation is key to their growth strategy. Curiosity plays a pivotal role in driving innovation and creative problem-solving.

- *Enhance employee engagement and satisfaction*: Gallup's State of the Global Workplace report reveals that highly engaged teams show 21% greater profitability. Curiosity-driven engagement initiatives have been linked to improved job satisfaction and retention.

- *Improve problem-solving skills and adaptability*: A research paper from MIT's Sloan School of Management highlights the correlation between curiosity and effective problem-solving. Employees who embrace curiosity are more adaptable and resilient in the face of challenges.

- *Develop leadership, communication, and teamwork abilities*: According to a study by the Center for Creative Leadership, leaders who exhibit curiosity are more likely to inspire and motivate their teams. Effective leadership, communication, and teamwork are all enhanced by a culture of curiosity.

- *Strengthen motivation and soft skills across the organization*: Research published in the *Journal of Applied Psychology* suggests that employees with strong soft skills, including emotional intelligence, are more likely to be motivated and to perform well. Curiosity-driven development programs can enhance these essential skills.

3. Understanding the Inhibitors

Provide an overview of fear, assumptions, technology, and environment as the primary barriers to curiosity. Briefly explain how each factor can limit curiosity and the importance of addressing them.

4. **Strategies to Overcome Fear**

Introduce practical exercises and workshops, such as failure workshops and fear-setting exercises, to reframe failure and manage anxiety. Highlight the importance of creating a supportive culture encouraging risk-taking and learning from mistakes.

5. **Challenging Assumptions**

Discuss the power of mindset workshops and the role of reflective journaling in challenging and changing limiting beliefs. Emphasize the importance of peer learning and sharing success stories to foster a growth mindset.

6. **Leveraging Technology Wisely**

Explore the dual role of technology in enhancing or hindering curiosity. Discuss strategies for appropriate technology use, including digital literacy workshops, tech-free brainstorming sessions, and leveraging technology for innovation.

7. **Creating a Supportive Environment**

Focus on the importance of psychological safety, diversity, and cross-functional collaboration in nurturing curiosity. Share strategies for building an environment that encourages experimentation, learning, and idea-sharing.

8. **Introducing Curiosity to Employees**

Outline the training program, including its structure and objectives. Highlight the significance of the FATE framework in understanding and developing curiosity.

9. **Action Plan & Commitment**

Conclude with a call to action for leaders to commit to fostering curiosity within their teams. Emphasize the importance of continued learning, experimentation, and celebrating curiosity. Include some final data to support the initiative.

- *Comprehensive training programs designed to foster curiosity*: PwC's 2021 Global Human Capital Trends report suggests that for every dollar invested in up-skilling employees, companies can expect a return of $2.30. Curiosity-focused training is a strategic investment in employee development.

- *Changes to the work environment that encourage questioning and exploration*: A study by Steelcase found that employees who had control over their workspace were 12% more satisfied with their jobs. Curiosity-friendly environments enhance job satisfaction and productivity.

- *Updates to policies that support curiosity and innovation*: McKinsey's research indicates that organizations that value and reward innovation are more likely to outperform their peers. Policy updates can incentivize curiosity-driven innovation.

- *Improved profit margin*: A study by Bersin, a research and advisory firm, found that organizations with mature learning and development programs have a 24% higher profit margin. Investing in a culture of curiosity aligns with organizational profitability and long-term success.

- *Summary*: A study by the *Harvard Business Review* emphasizes the importance of using data-driven metrics to assess the impact of culture change initiatives. Implementing CCI assessments aligns with best practices for measuring the success of a culture of curiosity.

Design each slide to facilitate engagement by incorporating visuals, stories, and data to make a compelling case for curiosity. Tailor the presentation to resonate with the leaders' goals and challenges, ensuring it drives home the message that cultivating curiosity is beneficial and essential for organizational growth and innovation.

Introducing Curiosity to Employees

Organizations usually provide a kickoff meeting to employees to introduce the culture of curiosity program, outlining objectives and sharing what's in it for them in order to generate enthusiasm.

Organizations can introduce the FATE framework and encourage icebreaker activities to foster networking. When training individuals, I have found that CCI-certified trainers often spend one day on each FATE factor, creating four half-day learning sessions. However, I have also succeeded in creating a half-day learning session to cover everything. The length usually depends on budgets, the size of the group, and the amount of change needed within the group. The presentation size can be adapted based on the time allotted for training.

To introduce the value of creating a culture of curiosity to the entire organization, consider the following slides:

1. **Introduction to Improving Curiosity to Overcome FATE**
   Begin with a welcome and explanation regarding how the program is designed to unlock curiosity and potential.

2. **Agenda Overview**
   Set a roadmap for the program.

3. **Why Curiosity?**
   Explain the value of curiosity for staying competitive, adaptable, engaged, and innovative.

4. **Icebreaker Activity**
   Set an activity to get to know each other better to set the tone for collaboration and openness.

5. **Introduction to Fear**
   Share a story about how fear creates a barrier.

6. **Impact of Fear on Curiosity**
   Explore how fears impact us and how to move beyond them.

7. **Failure Workshop**
   Share stories of failure and what can be learned from them.

8. **Fear-Setting Exercise**
   Envision worst-case scenarios and strategize how to mitigate the outcomes.

9. **Mindfulness Techniques**
   Practice mindful techniques that can keep us present and reduce anxiety.

10. **Scenario Simulation**

Role-play feared situations and develop strategies to face and overcome them.

11. **The Power of Assumptions**

Share the power of that voice in our heads.

12. **Assumption-Busting Session**

Confront assumptions and challenge what we think about ourselves and our capabilities.

13. **Growth Mindset Workshop**

Explore the fixed vs. growth mindset.

14. **Skill Expansion Projects**

Map out ideas or knowledge to explore with outlined challenges and opportunities.

15. **Navigating Technology**

Explore the over and under-utilization of technology.

16. **Digital Literacy**

Explore digital literacy and its impact on fueling curiosity and innovation.

17. **Tech-Free Think Tanks**

Brainstorm what tech-free days could entail and the outcomes from them.

18. **Tech Exploration**

Get hands-on with emerging technology.

19. **Cross-Functional Tech Teams**

Explain the value of collaboration across different areas of expertise.

20. **Creating a Curiosity-Friendly Environment**

Include strategies for creating spaces that inspire curiosity.

21. Psychological Safety

Share the value of psychological safety and the organization's plans to emulate what they want to see.

22. Innovation Labs and Creative Spaces

Share plans for physical or virtual spaces to work creatively and collaboratively.

23. Recognition and Rewards

Share the value of programs that reward curiosity and innovation.

24. Open Innovation Challenge

Plan an event that encourages creative problem-solving and innovation.

25. Recap and Reflection

Reflect on what was learned.

26. Commitment to Action

Commit to a culture of curiosity through action.

27. Closing

Thank them for their engagement and get them excited for the journey.

As with leader presentations, design each slide to facilitate engagement by incorporating visuals, stories, and data to make a compelling case for curiosity. Tailor the presentation to resonate with the employees' goals and challenges, ensuring it drives home the message that cultivating curiosity is beneficial and essential for organizational growth and innovation.

Overview of the activities involved in overcoming FATE:
We now know the value of curiosity, how it is impacted by things like fear, assumptions, technology, and the environment, and how it ultimately influences our happiness and productivity. We must create a growth mindset, set realistic goals, seek feedback, and take action to overcome those factors. We can best challenge our fears by journaling perceived failures and worst-case scenarios, seeking positive mentorship, and exploring strategies to mitigate these issues. By practicing active listening, asking questions, exposing ourselves to diverse perspectives, and embracing life-long learning, as well as uncertainty and ambiguity, we can challenge that voice of doubt in our minds. Set boundaries for over-use of technology, prioritize learning activities to embrace technology to augment our natural abilities, and stay informed of new technology to ensure no over or under-utilization of it occurs. To overcome environmental impacts, lead by example and encourage experimentation, promote psychological safety, and celebrate curiosity in yourself and others.

Fear:
Consider the following strategies and actions to overcome fear. Failure workshops can reframe our perception of success. To foster group discussions, analyze famous case studies of failure that led to success and ask what was learned and what themes and insights were gained. Inspired by Tim Ferriss's technique, use fear-setting exercises to construct "what if" and worst-case scenarios to reduce employee anxiety. When organizations create controlled environments to allow employees

to do things that generally cause fear—like public speaking or pitching new ideas—and provide constructive feedback with peer support groups, they can lessen employees' apprehension. Organizations can develop systems that reward risk-taking and resilience. When organizations celebrate stories and communicate highlights they can place value on bravery and curiosity. This should be a continuing process of initiatives spread over months, with regular adjustments based on feedback.

Assumptions:

Mindset workshops can help combat the limitations of assumptions. When employees learn about the value of facing the voice in their heads, they can recognize the unfounded beliefs that have limited them. Encouraging employees to undertake projects they usually would consider beyond their wheelhouse can encourage them to acquire new skills. Promoting reflective journaling can improve self-awareness and emotional intelligence, and facilitating peer learning sessions where employees can teach each other through exchanging ideas can support a learning culture and improve bias. Organizations must also create regular meetings to share success stories of overcoming assumptions. These strategies should be implemented slowly, incorporating more interactive and reflective exercises.

Technology:

It's critical that employees (and leaders) understand the dual role of technology. We want it to enhance our curiosity rather than replace it. Through digital learning workshops to help those overwhelmed by it, we can incorporate hands-on activities to explore the requisite tools. Having both high-tech and low-tech days can share the value of encouraging exploration and experimentation of technology and can enable brainstorming and problem-solving without technology. Organizations can identify projects that could benefit from different perspectives and leverage learning experimentation to encourage learning goals. Employees with strong tech skills can serve as mentors, while those with more technical skills might consider hosting hackathons to help solve business challenges. These strategies can leverage digital tools and foster innovation and continuous growth.

Environment:

Organizations should encourage leaders to model vulnerability and actively listen in order to cultivate psychological safety. Creating diverse teams and cross-pollinating ideas can help everyone challenge the status quo. Whiteboarding ideas and encouraging brainstorming sessions allow employees to share their perspectives in a safe environment. Offering subscriptions, lunch and learn sessions, innovation challenges, and flexible work arrangements can inspire people to be open to new possibilities. Encouraging employees to share new skills and learning can inspire others to do the same. Monitoring retention rates and employee satisfaction can help determine the program's impact.

Consider setting a 6-month goal to work on each of the factors of FATE:

- **MONTH 1: Identifying and Overcoming Fear**
  Begin by identifying personal and organizational fears that hinder curiosity. Engage in activities that encourage stepping out of comfort zones, such as participating in new projects or speaking up in meetings. Reflective journaling on these fears and how they affect daily work can help people to understand and gradually overcome them.

- **MONTH 2: Challenging Assumptions**
  Focus on recognizing and challenging the assumptions that limit curiosity. Implement a "question of the day" practice to stimulate thinking and question the status quo. Encourage team discussions to openly challenge and debate assumptions about work processes and practices.

- **MONTH 3: Optimal Use of Technology**
  Examine how the organization uses technology and identify ways it can hinder or enhance curiosity. Introduce "technology-free" periods to encourage face-to-face interactions and brainstorming sessions. Simultaneously, explore new technologies that can facilitate curiosity, such as collaboration tools or platforms for learning new skills.

- **MONTH 4: Enhancing the Environment**
  Modify the physical and cultural environment to foster curiosity. This could involve redesigning workspaces

to encourage collaboration or introducing curiosity corners where employees can share interesting finds or ideas. Cultivate a culture that recognizes and rewards curiosity.

- **MONTH 5: Integrating Curiosity into Daily Routines** Focus on embedding curiosity into the fabric of daily work life. Develop personal and team routines that encourage exploration and learning. This could include dedicating time for individual learning, team learning lunches, or "innovation hours" where employees can work on projects outside their usual scope.

- **MONTH 6: Reflection and Future Planning** Reflect on the progress made in fostering curiosity and plan future steps. Gather feedback from team members on the changes implemented and their impact on work practices. Set goals for continuous improvement and identify new areas in which to use curiosity. Throughout this plan, be open to feedback and be prepared to adjust strategies as needed. Regular check-ins and reflective practices will help track progress and ensure the journey toward embracing curiosity is ongoing and evolving.

CHAPTER 56

Kickbox

The value of an idea lies in the using of it.

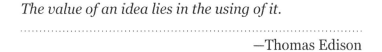

—Thomas Edison

Now that we know that curiosity sparks innovation, how do we bring our employees' innovative ideas into existence? One way is through a system designed by Mark Randall, Former VP of Creativity at Adobe, called Kickbox. In 2015, Randall created an open-sourced tool with materials that thousands of organizations have adapted to fit their needs.

What began as a two-day course for Adobe has blossomed into a toolkit that ignites curiosity and encourages innovation. The original Kickbox included a Starbucks gift card, templates, checklists, a six-stage process to get to a proof of concept, and a $1,000 prepaid credit card for employees (without needing receipts to get their idea past the usual corporate blockades). Previously, Adobe was prototyping 12 to 24 products each year, but during their first year using Kickbox, Adobe tested nearly 1,000 ideas for less money than they had spent to generate a dozen.

Randall expected that Kickbox would create many ideas, most of which would fail, but he reasoned that Adobe needed only one idea out of 1,000 to make the project worthwhile. Randall allowed anyone who wanted to innovate to attend workshops to share the Kickbox platform. This included administrative assistants, legal professionals—just about everyone. Randall was surprised to learn that when HR surveyed those who attended, they found that Kickbox was the highest-rated training program in the company's history. Kickbox enabled the company's more than 72,000 employees to learn startup development. Their initial challenge, which they called the Innovate Everywhere Challenge, was a huge success, with nearly half the organization participating and generating 1,100 new ideas.

To track Kickbox's success, Randall looked at the number of projects attempted rather than at the false positive results received from ideas that might have seemed initially reasonable but could have been more successful. He wanted to see early engagement indicators and believed $1,000 was a small investment considering the workshops and other costs employers often provide.

Kickbox's open-source mode enabled users to make suggestions. For instance, rather than having to come up with money to give employees to spend on their suggested ideas, they gave their employees tokens, where one token might be worth an hour of a programmer's time, for example.

Often, if you don't know what you don't know, you are more likely to be more creative since you lack an inner voice telling you that something can't be done. Kickbox's implementation yielded many prominent success stories, including Cisco's, which adapted it to fit their culture by renaming it Adventure

Kits, which generated thousands of new ideas. Some of Cisco's groundbreaking projects included LifeChanger and Rainmaker.

Organizations like 3M, Swisscom, and Roche, as well as educational institutions and government agencies, have also adopted it. Swisscom created a bottom-up intrapreneurship program that led to significant engagement.

Hundreds of startups from 27 countries applied for funding as part of Swisscom's Startup Challenge. The winners participated in an acceleration program at the Swisscom office in Silicon Valley, which gave them access to workshops, coaching, and more. Their success stories include Help2Type, creator of the first compact, haptic smartphone keyboard. And because Kickbox is open-source, organizations can adapt it to their culture, meaning that it can serve diverse sectors.

Implementing a supportive framework like Kickbox is important. Kickbox not only exemplifies how organizations can systematically address and overcome the impediments to curiosity but also highlights the tangible benefits of such endeavors: enhanced innovation, elevated employee engagement, and accelerated problem-solving capabilities. By integrating Kickbox or similar innovation-promoting tools into their culture, leaders can effectively transform their organizations into curiosity-driven powerhouses. This transformation goes beyond mere incremental improvements; it heralds a fundamental shift in how organizations approach challenges, devise solutions, and seize opportunities.

As organizations worldwide strive to stay relevant and competitive in an ever-evolving landscape, fostering a culture of curiosity through initiatives like Kickbox could very well be the linchpin in their strategy for sustainable growth and innovation.

CHAPTER 57

Involving Organizations

Be curious, not judgmental.

—Ted Lasso

When I was a doctoral chair, I guided doctoral students through their dissertations. I vividly recall one candidate who planned to explore curiosity's value to organizations and its impact on engagement. This research is crucial and many organizations could benefit from it, so I was disappointed when she chose a different path.

More published research is needed that quantifies the positive results organizations achieve when they embrace curiosity, which typically include increases in engagement, innovation, motivation, and productivity.

When initiating such a cultural change, leaders should first measure their employees' initial (baseline) curiosity levels. They can easily do this by using a quick assessment like the Five-Dimensional Curiosity Scale (5DC), created by Todd Kashdan et al., which is available online and below in the Appendix. (I am grateful to Todd for allowing me to include this in my book to make it easily accessible.)

The 5DC defines five curiosity dimensions: joyous exploration, deprivation sensitivity, stress tolerance, social curiosity, and thrill-seeking.

Organizations can customize their assessment to align with their desired outcomes. They can choose questions on the 5DC, like rating oneself on viewing challenging situations as opportunities to grow and learn, to tie into their current goals.

To measure engagement, organizations can use surveys like Gallup's. To ensure that financial outcomes improve, they can also use additional metrics such as sales and productivity.

Once they make baseline measurements, they can implement cultural change. I recommended they administer the Curiosity Code Index, which takes about 10 minutes and provides a report to use for training.

After undergoing the training outlined in the Curiosity Code Index chapter, organizations should set goals and objectives and then provide feedback to employees. After a period, typically six months or a year, employees should retake the 5DC and engagement surveys.

Analyzing the results allows organizations to identify correlations and can help them answer the following questions:

- Did employees' curiosity levels improve on the 5DC?
- Did their engagement levels increase according to the engagement survey?
- Did their productivity measurements improve?

The likely answer to all of the above is yes.

However, organizations must also track and publish these results. Because when they share their successes or failures, this contributes to research literature and helps facilitate further learning and growth across industries. This transparency also widely disseminates curiosity's impact on organizational success.

CONCLUSION

You have brains in your head. You have feet in your shoes. You can steer yourself in any direction you choose. You're on your own. And you know what you know. And YOU are the one who'll decide where to go.

—Dr. Seuss, Oh, The Places You'll Go!

I congratulate you for having had the curiosity to read this book! Take a moment to savor the pride of accomplishment and the excitement for what lies ahead. You've overcome challenges and fears, proving to yourself that curiosity can lead to extraordinary accomplishments.

In your curiosity journey, you've already exhibited courage by exploring the unknown, overcoming self-doubt, and pushing beyond the limits others might have set for you. Now, as you move forward, let your sense of curiosity guide you toward your passions.

Resist the urge to conform to societal expectations or to let others dictate your path. Embrace curiosity as a driving force in your life. Too many people merely exist; don't be like them and settle for a dull life devoid of curiosity. You've shown that you value curiosity; keep to the path you've started walking.

And it would have been easy to quit—but you didn't! Through perseverance, you've learned tenacity, understanding that hard work brings its own rewards. Some of you may have faced challenges and struggled, but view those struggles as valuable learning experiences. Thomas Edison's words resonate: "I have not failed. I've just found 10,000 ways that won't work." Embrace failure as a stepping stone to success.

Recognize the greatness within you. We often compare ourselves to others, thinking they possess more capabilities, but everyone has untapped potential. As current and future leaders, you need to cultivate empathy. Understand others' perspectives, ask questions, and show that you care about their experiences. We live in a diverse world, and curiosity is the key to building connections across differences.

In your future roles, whether as leaders or entrepreneurs, foster soft skills like empathy and compassion. Most people are hired for their knowledge and skills but are dismissed because of their behaviors. Be an example, mentor others, and embrace leaders who question the status quo. You've already demonstrated the ability to find a better way, and you are the architects of our future.

As we face new and unknown possibilities, Dr. Seuss's words remind us that we can shape our future. Developing curiosity in the workplace is not just a strategy, it is a declaration that we are the architects of our journey and, through curiosity, that we chart the course to undiscovered destinations.

Accept the challenge to do more and be more. Continue to change the course of history. Your journey has just begun, and I'm excited to witness the incredible impact you will make. Stay curious!

APPENDIX

Five-Dimensional Curiosity Scale Revised (5DCR)

Below are statements people often use to describe themselves. Please use the scale below to indicate the degree to which these statements accurately describe you. There are no right or wrong answers.

1 – Does not describe me at all
2 – Barely describes me
3 – Somewhat describes me
4 – Neutral
5 – Generally describes me
6 – Mostly describes me
7 – Completely describes me

Joyous Exploration:

1. I view challenging situations as an opportunity to grow and learn.
2. I seek out situations where it is likely that I will have to think in depth about something.
3. I enjoy learning about subjects that are unfamiliar to me.
4. I find it fascinating to learn new information.

Deprivation Sensitivity:

1. Thinking about solutions to difficult conceptual problems can keep me awake at night.
2. I can spend hours on a single problem because I just can't rest without knowing the answer.
3. I feel frustrated if I can't figure out the solution to a problem, so I work even harder to solve it.
4. I work relentlessly at problems that I feel must be solved.

Stress Tolerance: (entire subscale reverse-scored)

1. The smallest doubt can stop me from seeking out new experiences.
2. I cannot handle the stress that comes from entering uncertain situations.
3. I find it hard to explore new places when I lack confidence in my abilities.
4. It is difficult to concentrate when there is a possibility that I will be taken by surprise.

Thrill Seeking:

1. Risk-taking is exciting to me.
2. When I have free time, I want to do things that are a little scary.
3. Creating an adventure as I go is much more appealing than a planned adventure.
4. I prefer friends who are excitingly unpredictable.

Social Curiosity:
General Social Curiosity

1. I ask a lot of questions to figure out what interests other people.
2. When talking to someone who is excited, I am curious to find out why.
3. When talking to someone, I try to discover interesting details about them.
4. I like finding out why people behave the way they do.

Covert Social Curiosity

1. When other people are having a conversation, I like to find out what it's about.
2. When around other people, I like listening to their conversations.
3. When people quarrel, I like to know what's going on.
4. I seek out information about the private lives of people in my life.

Scoring instructions: Compute the average item score for each dimension and analyze separately (remember to reverse score Stress Tolerance items).

Kashdan, T.B., Disabato, D.J., Goodman, F.R., & McKnight, P.E. (in press). The Five-Dimensional Curiosity Scale Revised (5DCR): Briefer subscales while separating overt and covert social curiosity. *Personality and Individual Differences.*

Made in United States
North Haven, CT
11 November 2024

60130289R00173